G000090445

JD

JOHN DRYDEN

Selected Poems

BLOOMSBURY
* POETRY *
CLASSICS

This selection by Ian Hamilton first published 1994
Copyright © 1994 by Bloomsbury Publishing Ltd

Bloomsbury Publishing Ltd, 2 Soho Square,
London W1V 5DE

A CIP catalogue record for this book is available from the British
Library

ISBN 0 7475 1863 7

10 9 8 7 6 5 4 3 2 1

Typeset by Hewer Text Composition Services Limited,
Edinburgh
Printed in Great Britain by St Edmundsbury Press, Suffolk
Jacket design by Jeff Fisher

CONTENTS

From HEROIC STANZAS
[Written after Cromwell's Funeral]

And now 'tis time; for their officious haste
Who would before have borne him to the sky,
Like eager Romans, ere all rites were past,
Did let too soon the sacred eagle fly.

Though our best notes are treason to his fame
Joined with the loud applause of public voice,
Since heaven, what praise we offer to his name,
Hath rendered too authentic by its choice:

Though in his praise no arts can liberal be,
Since they whose muses have the highest flown
Add not to his immortal memory,
But do an act of friendship to their own:

Yet 'tis our duty and our interest too
Such monuments as we can build to raise,
Lest all the world prevent what we should do
And claim a title in him by their praise.

How shall I then begin or where conclude
To draw a fame so truly circular?
For in a round what order can be showed,
Where all the parts so equal-perfect are?

His grandeur he derived from heaven alone,
For he was great, ere fortune made him so;
And wars, like mists that rise against the sun,
Made him but greater seem, not greater grow.

No borrowed bays his temples did adorn,
But to our crown he did fresh jewels bring;
Nor was his virtue poisoned, soon as born,
With the too early thoughts of being king.

Fortune, that easy mistress of the young,
But to her ancient servants coy and hard,
Him at that age her favourites ranked among
When she her best-loved Pompey did discard.

He, private, marked the faults of others' sway
And set as sea-marks for himself to shun;
Not like rash monarchs, who their youth betray
By acts their age too late would wish undone.

And yet dominion was not his design;
We owe that blessing not to him but heaven,
Which to fair acts unsought rewards did join,
Rewards that less to him than us were given.

Our former chiefs, like sticklers of the war,
First sought to inflame the parties, then to poise.
The quarrel loved, but did the cause abhor,
And did not strike to hurt, but make a noise.

War, our consumption, was their gainful trade;
We inward bled, whilst they prolonged our pain:
He fought to end our fighting, and essayed
To stanch the blood by breathing of the vein.

Swift and resistless through the land he passed,
Like that bold Greek who did the East subdue,
And made to battles such heroic haste
As if on wings of victory he flew.

He fought, secure of fortune as of fame,
Till by new maps the island might be shown,
Of conquests, which he strewed where'er he came,
Thick as the galaxy with stars is sown.

His palms, though under weights they did not stand,
Still thrived; no winter could his laurels fade:
Heaven in his portrait showed a workman's hand
And drew it perfect, yet without a shade.

Peace was the prize of all his toils and care,
Which war had banished and did now restore:
Bologna's walls thus mounted in the air
To seat themselves more surely than before.

Her safety rescued Ireland to him owes;
And treacherous Scotland to no interest true,
Yet blessed that fate which did his arms dispose
Her land to civilize as to subdue.

Nor was he like those stars which only shine
When to pale mariners they storms portend;
He had his calmer influence, and his mien
Did love and majesty together blend.

* * *

Such was our prince; yet owned a soul above
The highest acts it could produce to show:
Thus poor mechanic arts in public move,
Whilst the deep secrets beyond practice go.

Nor died he when his ebbing fame went less,
But when fresh laurels courted him to live;
He seemed but to prevent some new success,
As if above what triumphs earth could give.

His latest victories still thickest came,
As near the centre motion does increase;
Till he, pressed down by his own weighty name,
Did, like the vestal, under spoils decease.

But first the ocean as a tribute sent
That giant-prince of all her watery herd;
And the isle, when her protecting genius went,
Upon his obsequies loud sighs conferred.

No civil broils have since his death arose,
But faction now by habit does obey;
And wars have that respect for his repose
As winds for halcyons when they breed at sea.

His ashes in a peaceful urn shall rest;
His name a great example stands to show
How strangely high endeavours may be blessed
Where piety and valour jointly go.

Now with a general peace the world was blessed,
While ours, a world divided from the rest,
A dreadful quiet felt, and worser far
Than arms, a sullen interval of war.
Thus when black clouds draw down the labouring
  skies,
Ere yet abroad the winged thunder flies,
A horrid stillness first invades the ear
And in that silence we the tempest fear.
The ambitious Swede, like restless billows tossed,
On this hand gaining what on that he lost,
Though in his life he blood and ruin breathed,
To his now guideless kingdom peace bequeathed;
And heaven that seemed regardless of our fate,
For France and Spain did miracles create,
Such mortal quarrels to compose in peace
As nature bred and interest did increase.
We sighed to hear the fair Iberian bride
Must grow a lily to the lily's side;
While our cross stars denied us Charles's bed,
Whom our first flames and virgin love did wed.
For his long absence church and state did groan;
Madness the pulpit, faction seized the throne:
Experienced age in deep despair was lost,
To see the rebel thrive, the loyal crossed:

Youth, that with joys had unacquainted been,
Envied grey hairs, that once good days had seen:
We thought our sires, not with their own content,
Had ere we came to age our portion spent.
Nor could our nobles hope their bold attempt
Who ruined crowns, would coronets exempt:
For when, by their designing leaders taught
To strike at power, which for themselves they sought,
The vulgar, gulled into rebellion, armed,
Their blood to action by the prize was warmed.
The sacred purple, then, and scarlet gown,
Like sanguine dye to elephants, was shown.
Thus when the bold Typhoeus scaled the sky
And forced great Jove from his own heaven to fly,
(What king, what crown, from treason's reach is free,
If Jove and heaven can violated be?)
The lesser gods that shared his prosperous state
All suffered in the exiled thunderer's fate.
The rabble now such freedom did enjoy,
As winds at sea that use it to destroy:
Blind as the Cyclops, and as wild as he,
They owned a lawless savage liberty,
Like that our painted ancestors so prized,
Ere empire's arts their breasts had civilized.
How great were then our Charles's woes, who thus
Was forced to suffer for himself and us!
He, tossed by fate, and hurried up and down,
Heir to his father's sorrows with his crown
Could taste no sweets of youth's desired age,

But found his life too true a pilgrimage
Unconquered yet in that forlorn estate,
His manly courage overcame his fate.
His wounds he took like Romans on his breast,
Which by his virtue were with laurels dressed.
As souls reach heaven, while yet in bodies pent,
So did he live above his banishment.
That sun which we beheld with cozened eyes
Within the water, moved along the skies.
How easy 'tis when destiny proves kind
With full-spread sails to run before the wind!
But those that 'gainst stiff gales laveering go,
Must be at once resolved, and skilful too.

* * *

And welcome now, great monarch, to your own!
Behold the approaching cliffs of Albion.
It is no longer motion cheats your view;
As you meet it, the land approacheth you.
The land returns, and in the white it wears
The marks of penitence and sorrow bears.
But you, whose goodness your descent doth show,
Your heavenly parentage and earthly too,
By that same mildness which your father's crown
Before did ravish, shall secure your own.
Not tied to rules of policy, you find
Revenge less sweet than a forgiving mind.
Thus when the almighty would to Moses give
A sight of all he could behold and live,
A voice before his entry did proclaim

Long-suffering, goodness, mercy, in his name.
Your power to justice doth submit your cause,
Your goodness only is above the laws;
Whose rigid letter, while pronounced by you,
Is softer made. So winds that tempests brew,
When through Arabian groves they take their flight,
Made wanton with rich odours, lose their spite.
And as those lees that trouble it refine
The agitated soul of generous wine;
So tears of joy, for your returning spilt,
Work out and expiate our former guilt.
Methinks I see those crowds on Dover's strand
Who in their haste to welcome you to land
Choked up the beach with their still growing store,
And made a wilder torrent on the shore:
While spurred with eager thoughts of past delight,
Those who had seen you court a second sight;
Preventing still your steps and making haste
To meet you often wheresoe'er you passed.
How shall I speak of that triumphant day,
When you renewed the expiring pomp of May!
(A month that owns an interest in your name:
You and the flowers are its peculiar claim.)
That star, that at your birth shone out so bright,
It stained the duller sun's meridian light,
Did once again its potent fires renew,
Guiding our eyes to find and worship you.

And now time's whiter series is begun,
Which in soft centuries shall smoothly run:
Those clouds that overcast your morn shall fly,
Dispelled to farthest corners of the sky.
Our nation, with united interest blest,
Not now content to poise, shall sway the rest.
Abroad your empire shall no limits know,
But like the sea in boundless circles flow;
Your much-loved fleet shall with a wide command
Besiege the petty monarchs of the land;
And as old time his offspring swallowed down,
Our ocean in its depths all seas shall drown.
Their wealthy trade from pirates' rapine free,
Our merchants shall no more adventurers be;
Nor in the farthest east those dangers fear,
Which humble Holland must dissemble here.
Spain to your gift alone her Indies owes;
For what the powerful takes not, he bestows:
And France that did an exile's presence fear,
May justly apprehend you still too near.
At home the hateful names of parties cease
And factious souls are wearied into peace.
The discontented now are only they
Whose crimes before did your just cause betray:
Of those your edicts some reclaim from sins,
But most your life and blest example wins.
Oh happy prince whom heaven hath taught the way
By paying vows to have more vows to pay!
Oh happy age! Oh times like those alone

By fate reserved for great Augustus' throne!
When the joint growth of arms and arts foreshow
The world a monarch, and that monarch you.

From AURENG-ZEBE
Prologue

Our Author by experience finds it true,
'Tis much more hard to please himself than you:
And you of no feign'd modesty, this day,
Damns his laborious Trifle of a Play:
Not that its worse than what before he writ,
But he has now another taste of Wit;
And to confess a truth, (though out of time)
Grows weary of his long-lov'd Mistris, Rhyme.
Passion's too fierce to be in Fetters bound,
And Nature flies him like Enchanted Ground.
What Verse can do, he has perform'd in this,
Which he presumes the most correct of his:
But spite of all his pride a secret shame,
Invades his breast at Shakespear's sacred name:
Aw'd when he hears his Godlike Romans rage,
He, in a just despair, would quit the Stage.
And to an Age less polish'd, more unskill'd,
Does, with disdain the foremost Honours yield.
As with the greater Dead he dares not strive,
He wou'd not match his Verse with those who live:
Let him retire, betwixt two Ages cast,
The first of this, and hindmost of the last.
A losing Gamester, let him sneak away;
He bears no ready Money from the Play.
The Fate which governs Poets, thought it fit,
He shou'd not raise his Fortunes by his Wit.

The Clergy thrive, and the litigious Bar:
Dull Heroes fatten with the spoils of War:
All Southern Vices, Heav'n be prais'd, are here;
But Wit's a luxury you think too dear.
When you to cultivate the Plant are loath,
'Tis a shrewed sign 'twas never of your growth:
And Wit in Northern Climates will not blow,
Except, like Orange-trees, 'tis hous'd from Snow.
There needs no care to put a Play-house down.
'Tis the most desart place of all the Town.
We and our Neighbours, to speak proudly, are
Like Monarchs, ruin'd with expensive War.
While, like wise English, unconcern'd, you sit.
And see us play the Tragedy of Wit.

From AURENG-ZEBE
Act IV, Sc. 1

When I consider Life, 'tis all a cheat;
Yet, fool'd with hope, men favour the deceit;
Trust on, and think tomorrow will repay:
Tomorrow's falser than the former day;
Lies worse; and while it says, We shall be blest
With some new joys, cuts off what we possest.
Strange couzenage! none would live past years again,
Yet all hope pleasure in what yet remain;
And, from the dregs of Life, think to receive
What the first sprightly running could not give.
I'm tir'd with waiting for this Chymic Gold,
Which fools us young, and beggars us when old.

MACFLECKNOE

All human things are subject to decay,
And when fate summons, monarchs must obey.
This Flecknoe found, who, like Augustus, young
Was called to empire, and had governed long;
In prose and verse, was owned, without dispute,
Through all the realms of Nonsense, absolute.
This aged prince, now flourishing in peace,
And blest with issue of a large increase,
Worn out with business, did at length debate
To settle the succession of the state;
And, pondering which of all his sons was fit
To reign, and wage immortal war with wit,
Cried: "'Tis resolved; for nature pleads, that he
Should only rule, who most resembles me.
Shadwell alone my perfect image bears,
Mature in dullness from his tender years:
Shadwell alone, of all my sons, is he
Who stands confirmed in full stupidity.
The rest to some faint meaning make pretence,
But Shadwell never deviates into sense.
Some beams of wit on other souls may fall,
Strike through, and make a lucid interval;
But Shadwell's genuine night admits no ray;
His rising fogs prevail upon the day.
Besides, his goodly fabric fills the eye,
And seems designed for thoughtless majesty;
Thoughtless as monarch oaks that shade the plain,

And, spread in solemn state, supinely reign.
Heywood and Shirley were but types of thee,
Thou last great prophet of tautology.
Even I, a dunce of more renown than they,
Was sent before but to prepare thy way:
And, coarsely clad in Norwich drugget, came
To teach the nations in thy greater name.
My warbling lute, the lute I whilom strung,
When to King John of Portugal I sung,
Was but the prelude to that glorious day,
When thou on silver Thames didst cut thy way,
With well-timed oars before the royal barge,
Swelled with the pride of thy celestial charge;
And big with hymn, commander of a host,
The like was ne'er in Epsom blankets tossed.
Methinks I see the new Arion sail,
The lute still trembling underneath thy nail.
At thy well-sharpened thumb from shore to shore
The treble squeaks for fear, the basses roar;
Echoes from Pissing Alley 'Shadwell' call,
And 'Shadwell' they resound from Ashton Hall.
About thy boat the little fishes throng.
As at the morning toast that floats along.
Sometimes, as prince of thy harmonious band,
Thou wield'st thy papers in thy threshing hand.
St. André's feet ne'er kept more equal time,
Not e'en the feet of thy own *Psyche's* rhyme;
Though they in number as in sense excel;
So just, so like tautology, they fell,

That, pale with envy, Singleton forswore
The lute and sword, which he in triumph bore,
And vowed he ne'er would act Villerius more.
Here stopped the good old sire, and wept for joy
In silent raptures of the hopeful boy.
All arguments, but most his plays, persuade,
That for anointed dullness he was made.

   Close to the walls which fair Augusta bind,
(The fair Augusta much to fears inclined,)
An ancient fabric raised to inform the sight,
There stood of yore, and Barbican it hight:
A watchtower once; but now, so fate ordains,
Of all the pile an empty name remains.
From its old ruins brothel-houses rise,
Scenes of lewd loves, and of polluted joys,
Where their vast courts the mother-strumpets keep,
And, undisturbed by watch, in silence sleep.
Near these a nursery erects its head,
Where queens are formed, and future heroes bred;
Where unfledged actors learn to laugh and cry,
Where infant punks their tender voices try,
And little Maximins the gods defy.
Great Fletcher never treads in buskins here,
Nor greater Jonson dares in socks appear;
But gentle Simkin just reception finds
Amidst this monument of vanished minds:
Pure clenches the suburban muse affords,
And Panton waging harmless war with words.
Here Flecknoe, as a place to fame well known,

Ambitiously designed his Shadwell's throne;
For ancient Dekker prophesied long since,
That in this pile should reign a mighty prince,
Born for a scourge of wit, and flail of sense;
To whom true dullness should some *Psyches* owe,
But worlds of *Misers* from his pen should flow;
Humourists and *Hypocrites* it should produce,
Whole Raymond families, and tribes of Bruce.
    Now Empress Fame had published the renown
Of Shadwell's coronation through the town.
Roused by report of Fame, the nations meet,
From near Bunhill, and distant Watling Street.
No Persian carpets spread the imperial way,
But scattered limbs of mangled poets lay;
From dusty shops neglected authors come,
Martyrs of pies, and relics of the bum.
Much Heywood, Shirley, Ogilby there lay,
But loads of Shadwell almost choked the way.
Bilked stationers for yeomen stood prepared,
And Herringman was captain of the guard.
The hoary prince in majesty appeared,
High on a throne of his own labours reared.
At his right hand our young Ascanius sate,
Rome's other hope, and pillar of the State.
His brows thick fogs, instead of glories, grace,
And lambent dullness played around his face.
As Hannibal did to the altars come,
Sworn by his sire a mortal foe to Rome;
So Shadwell swore, nor should his vow be vain,

That he till death true dullness would maintain;
And, in his father's right, and realm's defence,
Ne'er to have peace with wit, nor truce with sense.
The king himself the sacred unction made,
As king by office, and as priest by trade.
In his sinister hand, instead of ball,
He placed a mighty mug of potent ale;
Love's Kingdom to his right he did convey,
At once his sceptre, and his rule of sway;
Whose righteous lore the prince had practised young,
And from whose loins recorded *Psyche* sprung.
His temples, last, with poppies were o'erspread,
That nodding seemed to consecrate his head.
Just at that point of time, if fame not lie,
On his left hand twelve reverend owls did fly.
So Romulus, 'tis sung, by Tiber's brook,
Presage of sway from twice six vultures took.
The admiring throng loud acclamations make,
And omens of his future empire take.
The sire then shook the honours of his head,
And from his brows damps of oblivion shed
Full on the filial dullness: long he stood,
Repelling from his breast the raging god;
At length burst out in this prophetic mood:
  'Heavens bless my son, from Ireland let him reign
To far Barbadoes on the western main;
Of his dominion may no end be known,
And greater than his father's be his throne;
Beyond *Love's Kingdom* let him stretch his pen!'

He paused, and all the people cried, 'Amen.'
Then thus continued he: 'My son, advance
Still in new impudence, new ignorance.
Success let others teach, learn thou from me
Pangs without birth, and fruitless industry.
Let *Virtuosos* in five years be writ;
Yet not one thought accuse thy toil of wit.
Let gentle George in triumph tread the stage,
Make Dorimant betray, and Loveit rage;
Let Cully, Cockwood, Fopling, charm the pit,
And in their folly show the writer's wit.
Yet still thy fools shall stand in thy defence,
And justify their author's want of sense.
Let 'em be all by thy own model made
Of dullness, and desire no foreign aid;
That they to future ages may be known,
Not copies drawn, but issue of thy own.
Nay, let thy men of wit too be the same,
All full of thee, and differing but in name.
But let no alien Sedley interpose,
To lard with wit thy hungry *Epsom* prose.
And when false flowers of rhetoric thou wouldst cull,
Trust nature, do not labour to be dull;
But write thy best, and top; and, in each line,
Sir Formal's oratory will be thine:
Sir Formal, though unsought, attends thy quill,
And does thy northern dedications fill.
Nor let false friends seduce thy mind to fame,
By arrogating Jonson's hostile name.

Let father Flecknoe fire thy mind with praise,
And uncle Ogilby thy envy raise.
Thou art my blood, where Jonson has no part:
What share have we in nature, or in art?
Where did his wit on learning fix a brand,
And rail at arts he did not understand?
Where made he love in Prince Nicander's vein,
Or swept the dust in *Psyche's* humble strain?
Where sold he bargains, 'whip-stitch, kiss my arse',
Promised a play and dwindled to a farce?
When did his muse from Fletcher scenes purloin,
As thou whole Etherege dost transfuse to thine?
But so transfused, as oil on water's flow,
His always floats above, thine sinks below.
This is thy province, this thy wondrous way,
New humours to invent for each new play:
This is that boasted bias of thy mind,
By which one way, to dullness, 'tis inclined;
Which makes thy writings lean on one side still,
And, in all changes, that way bends thy will.
Nor let thy mountain-belly make pretence
Of likeness; thine's a tympany of sense.
A tun of man in thy large bulk is writ,
But sure thou'rt but a kilderkin of wit.
Like mine, thy gentle numbers feebly creep;
Thy tragic muse gives smiles, thy comic sleep.
With whate'er gall thou settst thyself to write,
Thy inoffensive satires never bite.
In thy felonious heart though venom lies,

It does but touch thy Irish pen, and dies.
Thy genius calls thee not to purchase fame
In keen iambics, but mild anagram.
Leave writing plays, and choose for thy command
Some peaceful province in acrostic land.
There thou mayst wings display and altars raise,
And torture one poor word ten thousand ways.
Or, if thou wouldst thy different talents suit,
Set thy own songs, and sing them to thy lute.'
   He said: but his last words were scarcely heard;
For Bruce and Longvil had a trap prepared,
And down they sent the yet declaiming bard.
Sinking he left his drugget robe behind,
Borne upwards by a subterranean wind.
The mantle fell to the young prophet's part,
With double portion of his father's art.

From ABSALOM AND ACHITOPHEL
Book One

In pious times, ere priestcraft did begin,
Before polygamy was made a sin;
When man on many multiplied his kind,
Ere one to one was cursedly confined;
When nature prompted, and no law denied
Promiscuous use of concubine and bride;
Then Israel's monarch after heaven's own heart,
His vigorous warmth did variously impart
To wives and slaves; and, wide as his command,
Scattered his maker's image through the land.
Michal, of royal blood, the crown did wear;
A soil ungrateful to the tiller's care:
Not so the rest; for several mothers bore
To godlike David several sons before.
But since like slaves his bed they did ascend,
No true succession could their seed attend.
Of all this numerous progeny was none
So beautiful, so brave, as Absalom:
Whether, inspired by some diviner lust,
His father got him with a greater gust;
Or that his conscious destiny made way,
By manly beauty, to imperial sway.
Early in foreign fields he won renown,
With kings and states allied to Israel's crown:
In peace the thoughts of war he could remove,
And seemed as he were only born for love.

Whate'er he did was done with so much ease,
In him alone 'twas natural to please:
His motions all accompanied with grace;
And paradise was opened in his face.
With secret joy indulgent David viewed
His youthful image in his son renewed:
To all his wishes nothing he denied,
And made the charming Annabel his bride.
What faults he had (for who from faults is free?)
His father could not, or he would not see.
Some warm excesses which the law forbore,
Were construed youth that purged by boiling o'er,
And Amnon's murder, by a specious name,
Was called a just revenge for injured fame.
Thus praised and loved the noble youth remained,
While David, undisturbed, in Sion reigned.
But life can never be sincerely blest;
Heaven punishes the bad, and proves the best.
The Jews, a headstrong, moody, murmuring race,
As ever tried the extent and stretch of grace;
God's pampered people, whom, debauched with ease,
No king could govern, nor no God could please
(Gods they had tried of every shape and size,
That god-smiths could produce, or priests devise);
These Adam-wits, too fortunately free,
Began to dream they wanted liberty;
And when no rule, no precedent was found,
Of men by laws less circumscribed and bound,
They led their wild desires to woods and caves,

And thought that all but savages were slaves.
They who, when Saul was dead, without a blow,
Made foolish Ishbosheth the crown forgo;
Who banished David did from Hebron bring,
And with a general shout proclaimed him king:
Those very Jews, who, at their very best,
Their humour more than loyalty expressed,
Now wondered why so long they had obeyed
An idol monarch, which their hands had made;
Thought they might ruin him they could create,
Or melt him to that golden calf, a state.
But these were random bolts; no formed design,
Nor interest made the factious crowd to join:
The sober part of Israel, free from stain,
Well knew the value of a peaceful reign,
And, looking backward with a wise affright,
Saw seams of wounds, dishonest to the sight:
In contemplation of whose ugly scars
They cursed the memory of civil wars.
The moderate sort of men, thus qualified,
Inclined the balance to the better side;
And David's mildness managed it so well,
The bad found no occasion to rebel.
But when to sin our biased nature leans,
The careful devil is still at hand with means;
And providently pimps for ill desires.
The Good Old Cause revived, a plot requires:
Plots, true or false, are necessary things,
To raise up commonwealths, and ruin kings.

The inhabitants of old Jerusalem
Were Jebusites, the town so called from them;
And theirs the native right –
But when the chosen people grew more strong,
The rightful cause at length became the wrong;
And every loss the men of Jebus bore,
They still were thought God's enemies the more.
Thus worn and weakened, well or ill content,
Submit they must to David's government:
Impoverished and deprived of all command,
Their taxes doubled as they lost their land;
And what was harder yet to flesh and blood,
Their gods disgraced, and burnt like common wood.
This set the heathen priesthood in a flame;
For priests of all religions are the same:
Of whatsoe'er descent their godhead be,
Stock, stone, or other homely pedigree,
In his defence his servants are as bold,
As if he had been born of beaten gold.
The Jewish rabbins, though their enemies,
In this conclude them honest men and wise:
For 'twas their duty, all the learned think,
To espouse his cause, by whom they eat and drink.
From hence began that Plot, the nation's curse,
Bad in itself, but represented worse;
Raised in extremes, and in extremes decried;
With oaths affirmed, with dying vows denied.
Not weighed or winnowed by the multitude;
But swallowed in the mass, unchewed and crude.

Some truth there was, but dashed and brewed with lies,
To please the fools, and puzzle all the wise.
Succeeding times did equal folly call,
Believing nothing, or believing all.
The Egyptian rites the Jebusites embraced;
Where gods were recommended by their taste.
Such savoury deities must needs be good,
As served at once for worship and for food.
By force they could not introduce these gods,
For ten to one in former days was odds;
So fraud was used (the sacrificer's trade):
Fools are more hard to conquer than persuade.
Their busy teachers mingled with the Jews,
And raked for converts even the court and stews:
Which Hebrew priests the more unkindly took,
Because the fleece accompanies the flock.
Some thought they God's anointed meant to slay
By guns, invented since full many a day:
Our author swears it not; but who can know
How far the Devil and Jebusites may go?
This Plot, which failed for want of common sense,
Had yet a deep and dangerous consequence:
For, as when raging fevers boil the blood,
The standing lake soon floats into a flood,
And every hostile humour, which before
Slept quiet in its channels, bubbles o'er;
So several factions from this first ferment
Work up to foam, and threat the government.
Some by their friends, more by themselves thought wise,

Opposed the power to which they could not rise.
Some had in courts been great, and thrown from
   thence,
Like fiends were hardened in impenitence.
Some, by their monarch's fatal mercy, grown
From pardoned rebels kinsmen to the throne,
Were raised in power and public office high;
Strong bands, if bands ungrateful men could tie.
   Of these the false Achitophel was first,
A name to all succeeding ages cursed:
For close designs and crooked counsels fit;
Sagacious, bold, and turbulent of wit;
Restless, unfixed in principles and place;
In power unpleased, impatient of disgrace:
A fiery soul, which, working out its way,
Fretted the pigmy body to decay,
And o'er-informed the tenement of clay.
A daring pilot in extremity;
Pleased with the danger, when the waves went
   high,
He sought the storms; but, for a calm unfit,
Would steer too nigh the sands, to boast his wit.
Great wits are sure to madness near allied,
And thin partitions do their bounds divide;
Else why should he, with wealth and honour blest,
Refuse his age the needful hours of rest?
Punish a body which he could not please;
Bankrupt of life, yet prodigal of ease?
And all to leave what with his toil he won,

To that unfeathered two-legged thing, a son,
Got, while his soul did huddled notions try;
And born a shapeless lump, like anarchy.
In friendship false, implacable in hate;
Resolved to ruin or to rule the state.
To compass this the triple bond he broke,
The pillars of the public safety shook;
And fitted Israel for a foreign yoke:
Then seized with fear, yet still affecting fame,
Usurped a patriot's all-atoning name.
So easy still it proves in factious times,
With public zeal to cancel private crimes.
Who think too little, and who talk too much.
These, out of mere instinct, they knew not why,
Adored their fathers' God and property;
And, by the same blind benefit of fate,
The devil and the Jebusite did hate:
Born to be saved, e'en in their own despite,
Because they could not help believing right.

* * *

Such were the tools; but a whole Hydra more
Remains, of spouting heads too long to score.

Some of their chiefs were princes of the land:
In the first rank of these did Zimri stand;
A man so various, that he seemed to be
Not one, but all mankind's epitome:
Stiff in opinions, always in the wrong;
Was everything by starts, and nothing long;
But, in the course of one revolving moon,

Was chemist, fiddler, statesman, and buffoon:
Then all for women, painting, rhyming, drinking,
Besides ten thousand freaks that died in thinking.
Blest madman, who could every hour employ,
With something new to wish, or to enjoy!
Railing and praising were his usual themes;
And both (to show his judgment) in extremes:
So over-violent, or over-civil,
That every man, with him, was God or devil.
In squandering wealth was his peculiar art:
Nothing went unrewarded but desert.
Beggared by fools, whom still he found too late,
He had his jest, and they had his estate.
He laughed himself from court; then sought relief
By forming parties, but could ne'er be chief;
For, spite of him, the weight of business fell
On Absalom and wise Achitophel:
Thus, wicked but in will, of means bereft,
He left not faction, but of that was left.

From ABSALOM AND ACHITOPHEL
Book Two

Now stop your noses, readers, all and some,
For here's a tun of midnight work to come,
Og, from a treason-tavern rolling home
Round as a globe, and liquored every chink,
Goodly and great he sails behind his link.
With all this bulk there's nothing lost in Og,
For every inch that is not fool is rogue:
A monstrous mass of foul corrupted matter,
As all the devils had spewed to make the batter.
When wine has given him courage to blaspheme,
He curses God, but God before cursed him;
And if man could have reason, none has more,
That made his paunch so rich, and him so poor.
With wealth he was not trusted, for heaven knew
What 'twas of old to pamper up a Jew;
To what would he on quail and pheasant swell,
That e'en on tripe and carrion could rebel?
But though heaven made him poor (with reverence
  speaking),
He never was a poet of God's making.
The midwife laid her hand on his thick skull,
With this prophetic blessing: *be thou dull*;
Drink, swear, and roar, forbear no lewd delight
Fit for thy bulk, do anything but write:
Thou art of lasting make, like thoughtless men,
A strong nativity – but for the pen;

Eat opium, mingle arsenic in thy drink,
Still thou mayst live, avoiding pen and ink.
I see, I see, 'tis counsel given in vain,
For treason botched in rhyme will be thy bane;
Rhyme is the rock on which thou art to wreck,
'Tis fatal to thy fame and to thy neck:
Why should thy metre good King David blast?
A psalm of his will surely be thy last.
Darest thou presume in verse to meet thy foes,
Thou whom the penny pamphlet foiled in prose?
Doeg, whom God for mankind's mirth has made,
O'ertops thy talent in thy very trade;
Doeg to thee, thy paintings are so coarse,
A poet is, though he's the poets' horse.
A double noose thou on thy neck dost pull,
For writing treason, and for writing dull;
To die for faction is a common evil,
But to be hanged for nonsense is the devil:
Hadst thou the glories of thy king expressed,
Thy praises had been satire at the best;
But thou in clumsy verse, unlicked, unpointed,
Hast shamefully defied the Lord's anointed:
I will not rake the dunghill of thy crimes,
For who would read thy life that reads thy rhymes?
But of King David's foes, be this the doom,
May all be like the young man Absalom;
And for my foes may this their blessing be,
To talk like Doeg, and to write like thee.

A SONG FOR ST CECILIA'S DAY, 1687

I

From harmony, from heavenly harmony,
    This universal frame began:
  When nature underneath a heap
    Of jarring atoms lay,
  And could not heave her head,
The tuneful voice was heard from high,
    'Arise, ye more than dead.'
Then cold, and hot, and moist, and dry,
In order to their stations leap,
    And Music's power obey.
From harmony, from heavenly harmony,
    This universal frame began;
    From harmony to harmony
Through all the compass of the notes it ran,
The diapason closing full in man.

II

What passion cannot music raise and quell?
    When Jubal struck the corded shell,
  His listening brethren stood around,
  And, wondering, on their faces fell
  To worship that celestial sound:
Less than a God they thought there could not dwell
    Within the hollow of that shell
    That spoke so sweetly and so well.
What passion cannot music raise the quell?

III

The trumpet's loud clangour
    Excites us to arms,
With shrill notes of anger
    And mortal alarms.
The double double double beat
    Of the thundering drum,
Cries 'hark! the foes come:
Charge, charge! 'tis too late to retreat.'

IV

The soft complaining flute,
In dying notes discovers
The woes of hopeless lovers;
Whose dirge is whispered by the warbling lute.

V

Sharp violins proclaim
Their jealous pangs, and desperation,
Fury, frantic indignation,
Depth of pains, and height of passion,
    For the fair, disdainful dame.

VI

But, oh! what art can teach,
    What human voice can reach,
The sacred organ's praise?
Notes inspiring holy love,
Notes that wing their heavenly ways
    To mend the choirs above.

VII

Orpheus could lead the savage race;
And trees unrooted left their place,
   Sequacious of the lyre:
But bright Cecilia raised the wonder higher;
When to her organ vocal breath was given,
An angel heard, and straight appeared,
   Mistaking earth for heaven.

Grand Chorus

As from the power of sacred lays
   The spheres began to move,
And sung the great creator's praise
   To all the blessed above;
So when the last and dreadful hour
This crumbling pageant shall devour,
The trumpet shall be heard on high,
The dead shall live, the living die,
And Music shall untune the sky.

From RELIGIO LAICI

Dim as the borrowed beams of moon and stars
To lonely, weary, wandering travellers,
Is reason to the soul; and, as on high
Those rolling fires discover but the sky,
Not light us here, so reason's glimmering ray
Was lent, not to assure our doubtful way,
But guide us upward to a better day.
And as those nightly tapers disappear,
When day's bright lord ascends our hemisphere;
So pale grows reason at religion's sight;
So dies, and so dissolves in supernatural light.
Some few, whose lamp shone brighter, have been led
From cause to cause, to nature's secret head;
And found that one first principle must be:
But what, or who, that UNIVERSAL HE;
Whether some soul encompassing this ball,
Unmade, unmoved, yet making, moving all;
Or various atoms' interfering dance
Leapt into form, the noble work of chance;
Or this great all was from eternity;
Not e'en the Stagirite himself could see,
And Epicurus guessed as well as he.
As blindly groped they for a future state;
As rashly judged of providence and fate:
But least of all could their endeavours find
What most concerned the good of humankind;
For happiness was never to be found,

42

But vanished from 'em like enchanted ground.
One thought content the good to be enjoyed;
This every little accident destroyed;
The wiser madmen did for virtue toil,
A thorny, or at best a barren soil;
In pleasure some their glutton souls would steep,
But found their line too short, the well too deep,
And leaky vessels which no bliss could keep.
Thus anxious thoughts in endless circles roll,
Without a centre where to fix the soul;
In this wild maze their vain endeavours end:
How can the less the greater comprehend?
Or finite reason reach infinity?
For what could fathom God were more than he.

* * *

In times o'ergrown with rust and ignorance,
A gainful trade their clergy did advance;
When want of learning kept the laymen low,
And none but priests were authorized to know;
When what small knowledge was, in them did dwell,
And he a god who could but read or spell:
Then mother church did mightily prevail;
She parcelled out the Bible by retail;
But still expounded what she sold or gave,
To keep it in her power to damn and save:
Scripture was scarce, and, as the market went,
Poor laymen took salvation on content;
As needy men take money, good or bad:
God's word they had not, but the priest's they had.

Yet, whate'er false conveyances they made,
The lawyer still was certain to be paid.
In those dark times they learned their knack so well,
That by long use they grew infallible:
At last, a knowing age began to enquire
If they the book, or that did them inspire;
And, making narrower search, they found, though
    late,
That what they thought the priest's was their estate,
Taught by the will produced (the written word)
How long they had been cheated on record.
Then every man who saw the title fair
Claimed a child's part, and put in for a share;
Consulted soberly his private good,
And saved himself as cheap as e'er he could.

  'Tis true, my friend (and far be flattery hence),
This good had full as bad a consequence:
The book thus put in every vulgar hand,
Which each presumed he best could understand,
The common rule was made the common prey,
And at the mercy of the rabble lay.
The tender page with horny fists was galled,
And he was gifted most that loudest bawled:
The Spirit gave the doctoral degree;
And every member of a Company
Was of his trade and of the Bible free.
Plain truths enough for needful use they found,
But men would still be itching to expound:
Each was ambitious of the obscurest place,

No measure ta'en from knowledge, all from Grace.
Study and pains were now no more their care;
Texts were explained by fasting and by prayer:
This was the fruit the private spirit brought,
Occasioned by great zeal and little thought.
While crowds unlearned, with rude devotion warm,
About the sacred viands buzz and swarm,
The fly-blown text creates a crawling brood,
And turns to maggots what was meant for food.
A thousand daily sects rise up and die;
A thousand more the perished race supply:
So all we make of heaven's discovered will
Is, not to have it, or to use it ill.
The danger's much the same; on several shelves
If others wreck us, or we wreck ourselves.
    What then remains, but, waiving each extreme,
The tides of ignorance and pride to stem?
Neither so rich a treasure to forgo,
Nor proudly seek beyond our power to know.
Faith is not built on disquisitions vain;
The things we must believe are few and plain:
But since men will believe more than they need,
And every man will make himself a creed,
In doubtful questions 'tis the safest way
To learn what unsuspected ancients say;
For 'tis not likely we should higher soar
In search of heaven, than all the church before;
Nor can we be deceived, unless we see
The scripture and the Fathers disagree.

If, after all, they stand suspected still
(For no man's faith depends upon his will),
'Tis some relief that points not clearly known
Without much hazard may be let alone:
And after hearing what our church can say,
If still our reason runs another way,
That private reason 'tis more just to curb,
Than by disputes the public peace disturb.
For points obscure are of small use to learn;
But common quiet is mankind's concern.

    Thus have I made my own opinions clear;
Yet neither praise expect, nor censure fear:
And this unpolished, rugged verse, I chose,
As fittest for discourse, and nearest prose;
For while from sacred truth I do not swerve,
Tom Sternhold's, or Tom Shadwell's rhymes will serve.

From THE HIND AND THE PANTHER

What weight of antient witness can prevail
If private reason hold the publick scale?
But, gratious God, how well dost thou provide
For erring judgments an unerring Guide?
Thy throne is darkness in th' abyss of light,
A blaze of glory that forbids the sight;
O teach me to believe Thee thus conceal'd,
And search no farther than thy self reveal'd;
But her alone for my Directour take
Whom thou hast promis'd never to forsake!
My thoughtless youth was wing'd with vain desires,
My manhood, long misled by wandering fires,
Follow'd false lights; and when their glimps was gone,
My pride struck out new sparkles of her own.
Such was I, such by nature still I am,
Be thine the glory, and be mine the shame.
Good life be now my task: my doubts are done,
(What more could fright my faith, than Three in
    One?)
Can I believe eternal God could lye
Disguis'd in mortal mold and infancy?
That the great maker of the world could dye?
And after that, trust my imperfect sense
Which calls in question his omnipotence?
Can I my reason to my faith compell,
And shall my sight, and touch, and taste rebell?
Superiour faculties are set aside,

Shall their subservient organs be my guide?
Then let the moon usurp the rule of day,
And winking tapers shew the sun his way;
For what my senses can themselves perceive
I need no revelation to believe.

TO MY DEAR FRIEND MR CONGREVE

Well then, the promised hour is come at last,
The present age of wit obscures the past.
Strong were our sires, and as they fought they writ,
Conquering with force of arms and dint of wit:
Theirs was the giant race before the flood;
And thus, when Charles returned, our empire stood.
Like Janus he the stubborn soil manured,
With rules of husbandry the rankness cured;
Tamed us to manners when the stage was rude,
And boisterous English wit with art endued.
Our age was cultivated thus at length;
But what we gained in skill we lost in strength.
Our builders were with want of genius cursed;
The second temple was not like the first;
Till you, the best Vitruvius, come at length,
Our beauties equal, but excel our strength.
Firm doric pillars found your solid base;
The fair corinthian crowns the higher space:
Thus all below is strength, and all above is grace.
In easy dialogue is Fletcher's praise;
He moved the mind, but had not power to raise.
Great Jonson did by strength of judgment please;
Yet doubling Fletcher's force, he wants his ease.
In differing talents both adorned their age;
One for the study, t' other for the stage.
But both to Congreve justly shall submit,
One matched in judgment, both o'ermatched in wit.

In him all beauties of this age we see,
Etherege's courtship, Southerne's purity,
The satire, wit, and strength, of manly Wycherley.
All this in blooming youth you have achieved,
Nor are your foiled contemporaries grieved.
So much the sweetness of your manners move,
We cannot envy you, because we love.
Fabius might joy in Scipio, when he saw
A beardless consul made against the law,
And join his suffrage to the votes of Rome,
Though he with Hannibal was overcome.
Thus old Romano bowed to Raphael's fame,
And scholar to the youth he taught became.

O that your brows my laurel had sustained,
Well had I been deposed, if you had reigned!
The father had descended for the son;
For only you are lineal to the throne.
Thus when the state one Edward did depose,
A greater Edward in his room arose:
But now not I, but poetry, is cursed;
For Tom the second reigns like Tom the first.
But let them not mistake my patron's part,
Nor call his charity their own desert
Yet this I prophesy; thou shalt be seen,
(Though with some short parenthesis between,)
High on the throne of wit, and, seated there,
Not mine (that's little) but thy laurel wear.
Thy first attempt an early promise made;
That early promise this has more than paid.

So bold, yet so judiciously you dare
That your least praise is to be regular.
Time, place, and action may with pains be wrought,
But genius must be born and never can be taught.
This is your portion, this your native store.
Heaven, that but once was prodigal before,
To Shakespeare gave as much, he could not give him
  more.
  Maintain your post; that's all the fame you need;
For 'tis impossible you should proceed.
Already I am worn with cares and age,
And just abandoning the ungrateful stage;
Unprofitably kept at heaven's expense,
I live a rent-charge on his providence:
But you, whom every muse and grace adorn,
Whom I foresee to better fortune born,
Be kind to my remains; and oh, defend,
Against your judgment, your departed friend!
Let not the insulting foe my fame pursue,
But shade those laurels which descend to you;
And take for tribute what these lines express:
You merit more, nor could my love do less.

TO THE MEMORY OF MR OLDHAM

Farewell, too little and too lately known,
Whom I began to think and call my own;
For sure our souls were near allied; and thine
Cast in the same poetic mould with mine.
One common note on either lyre did strike,
And knaves and fools we both abhorred alike:
To the same goal did both our studies drive,
The last set out the soonest did arrive.
Thus Nisus fell upon the slippery place,
While his young friend performed and won the race.
O early ripe – to thy abundant store
What could advancing age have added more?
It might (what nature never gives the young)
Have taught the numbers of thy native tongue.
But satire needs not those, and wit will shine
Through the harsh cadence of a rugged line:
A noble error, and but seldom made,
When poets are by too much force betrayed.
Thy generous fruits, though gathered ere their prime
Still showed a quickness; and maturing time
But mellows what we write to the dull sweets of
    rhyme.
Once more, hail and farewell; farewell thou young
But ah too short, Marcellus of our tongue;
Thy brows with ivy, and with laurels bound;
But fate and gloomy night encompass thee around.

AN ODE ON THE DEATH OF MR HENRY PURCELL

I

Mark how the lark and linnet sing;
           With rival notes
       They strain their warbling throats,
           To welcome in the spring.
           But in the close of night,
       When Philomel begins her heavenly lay,
           They cease their mutual spite,
       Drink in her music with delight,
And, listening and silent and silent and listening,
       and listening and silent obey.

II

So ceased the rival crew when Purcell came;
They sang no more, or only sang his fame.
Struck dumb, they all admired the godlike man:
           The goodlike man,
           Alas! too soon retired,
           As he too late began.
We beg not hell our Orpheus to restore;
       Had he been there,
       Their sovereigns' fear
       Had sent him back before.
The power of harmony too well they know:
He long ere this had tuned their jarring sphere,
       And left no hell below.

III

The heavenly choir, who heard his notes from high,
Let down the scale of music from the sky;
      They handed him along,
And all the way he taught, and all the way they sung.
    Ye brethren of the lyre, and tuneful voice,
    Lament his lot, but at your own rejoice:
Now live secure, and linger out your days;
The gods are pleased alone with Purcell's lays,
      Nor know to mend their choice.

A SONG TO A FAIR YOUNG LADY GOING OUT OF TOWN IN THE SPRING

Ask not the cause why sullen spring
 So long delays her flowers to bear;
Why warbling birds forget to sing,
 And winter storms invert the year.
Chloris is gone, and fate provides
To make it spring where she resides.

Chloris is gone, the cruel fair;
 She cast not back a pitying eye;
But left her lover in despair,
 To sigh, to languish, and to die.
Ah, how can those fair eyes endure,
To give the wounds they will not cure!

Great god of love, why hast thou made
 A face that can all hearts command,
That all religions can invade,
 And change the laws of every land?
Where thou hadst placed such power before,
Thou shouldst have made her mercy more.

When Chloris to the temple comes,
 Adoring crowds before her fall;
She can restore the dead from tombs,
 And every life but mine recall.
I only am, by love, designed
To be the victim for mankind.

A SONG

Fair, sweet, and young, receive a prize
Reserved for your victorious eyes:
From crowds, whom at your feet you see,
O pity, and distinguish me!
As I from thousand beauties more
Distinguish you, and only you adore.

Your face for conquest was designed,
Your every motion charms my mind:
Angels, when you your silence break,
Forget their hymns, to hear you speak;
But when at once they hear and view,
Are loath to mount, and long to stay with you.

No graces can your form improve,
But all are lost, unless you love;
While that sweet passion you disdain,
Your veil and beauty are in vain.
In pity then prevent my fate,
For after dying all reprieve's too late.

From CYMON AND IPHIGENIA

Old as I am, for ladies' love unfit,
The power of beauty I remember yet,
Which once inflamed my soul, and still inspires my
 wit.
If love be folly, the severe divine
Has felt that folly, though he censures mine;
Pollutes the pleasures of a chaste embrace,
Acts what I write, and propagates in grace
With riotous excess, a priestly race.
Suppose him free, and that I forge the offence,
He showed the way, perverting first my sense:
In malice witty, and with venom fraught,
He makes me speak the things I never thought.
Compute the gains of his ungoverned zeal;
Ill suits his cloth the praise of railing well.
The world will think that what we loosely write,
Though now arraigned, he read with some delight;
Because he seems to chew the cud again,
When his broad comment makes the text too plain:
And teaches more in one explaining page,
Than all the double meanings of the stage.
 What needs he paraphrase on what we mean?
We were at worst but wanton; he's obscene.
I, nor my fellows, nor myself excuse;
But love's the subject of the comic muse:
Nor can we write without it, nor would you
A tale of only dry instruction view;

Nor love is always of a vicious kind,
But oft to virtuous acts inflames the mind.
Awakes the sleepy vigour of the soul,
And, brushing o'er, adds motion to the pool.
Love, studious how to please, improves our parts
With polished manners, and adorns with arts.
Love first invented verse, and formed the rhyme,
The motion measured, harmonized the chime;
To liberal acts enlarged the narrow-souled,
Softened the fierce, and made the coward bold;
The world when waste, he peopled with increase,
And warring nations reconciled in peace.
Ormonde, the first, and all the fair may find,
In this one legend to their fame designed,
When beauty fires the blood, how love exalts the mind.

In that sweet isle, where Venus keeps her court,
And every grace and all the loves resort;
Where either sex is formed of softer earth,
And takes the bent of pleasure from their birth;
There lived a Cyprian lord, above the rest,
Wise, wealthy, with a numerous issue blessed.
    But as no gift of fortune is sincere,
Was only wanting in a worthy heir:
His eldest born a goodly youth to view
Excelled the rest in shape, and outward show;
Fair, tall, his limbs with due proportion joined,
But of a heavy, dull, degenerate mind.
His soul belied the features of his face;

Beauty was there, but beauty in disgrace.
A clownish mien, a voice with rustic sound,
And stupid eyes, that ever loved the ground.
He looked like nature's error; as the mind
And body were not of a piece designed,
But made for two, and by mistake in one were joined.

The ruling rod, the father's forming care,
Were exercised in vain, on wit's despair;
The more informed the less he understood,
And deeper sunk by floundering in the mud.
Now scorned of all and grown the public shame,
The people from Galesus changed his name,
And Cymon called, which signifies a brute;
So well his name did with his nature suit.

His father, when he found his labour lost,
And care employed, that answered not the cost,
Chose an ungrateful object to remove,
And loathed to see what nature made him love;
So to his country farm the fool confined:
Rude work well suited with a rustic mind.
Thus to the wilds the sturdy Cymon went,
A squire among the swains, and pleased with
    banishment.
His corn and cattle were his only care,
And his supreme delight a country fair.

It happened on a summer's holiday,
That to the greenwood shade he took his way;
For Cymon shunned the church, and used not much
    to pray.

His quarter-staff, which he could ne'er forsake,
Hung half before, and half behind his back.
He trudged along unknowing what he sought,
And whistled as he went, for want of thought.

By chance conducted, or by thirst constrained,
The deep recesses of the grove he gained;
Where in a plain, defended by the wood,
Crept through the matted grass a crystal flood,
By which an alabaster fountain stood:
And on the margin of the fount was laid,
Attended by her slaves, a sleeping maid.
Like Dian, and her nymphs, when tired with sport,
To rest by cool Eurotas they resort.
The dame herself the goddess well expressed,
Not more distinguished by her purple vest,
Than by the charming features of her face,
And e'en in slumber a superior grace:
Her comely limbs composed with decent care,
Her body shaded with a slight cymar;
Her bosom to the view was only bare:
Where two beginning paps were scarcely spied,
For yet their places were but signified:
The fanning wind upon her bosom blows,
To meet the fanning wind the bosom rose;
The fanning wind and purling streams continue her
    repose.

The fool of nature stood with stupid eyes
And gaping mouth, that testified surprise,
Fixed on her face, nor could remove his sight

New as he was to love, and novice in delight:
Long mute he stood, and leaning on his staff,
His wonder witnessed with an idiot laugh;
Then would have spoke, but by his glimmering sense
First found his want of words, and feared offence:
Doubted for what he was he should be known,
By his clown accent, and his country tone.

Through the rude chaos thus the running light
Shot the first ray that pierced the native night:
Then day and darkness in the mass were mixed,
Till gathered in a globe, the beams were fixed:
Last shone the sun who radiant in his sphere
Illumined heaven and earth, and rolled around the
    year.
So reason in this brutal soul began:
Love made him first suspect he was a man;
Love made him doubt his broad barbarian sound,
By love his want of words, and wit he found:
That sense of want prepared the future way
To knowledge, and disclosed the promise of a day.

What not his father's care, nor tutor's art
Could plant with pains in his unpolished heart,
The best instructor, love at once inspired,
As barren grounds to fruitfulness are fired;
Love taught him shame, and shame with love at strife
Soon taught the sweet civilities of life.
His gross material soul at once could find
Somewhat in her excelling all her kind;
Exciting a desire till then unknown,

Somewhat unfound, or found in her alone.
This made the first impression in his mind,
Above, but just above, the brutal kind.
For beasts can like, but not distinguish too,
Nor their own liking by reflection know;
Nor why they like or this or t'other face,
Or judge of this or that peculiar grace;
But love in gross, and stupidly admire;
As flies, allured by light, approach the fire.
Thus our man-beast, advancing by degrees,
First likes the whole, then separates what he sees;
On several parts a several praise bestows,
The ruby lips, the well-proportioned nose,
The snowy skin, the raven-glossy hair,
The dimpled cheek, the forehead rising fair,
And e'en in sleep itself a smiling air.
From thence his eyes descending viewed the rest,
Her plump round arms, white hands, and heaving
    breast.
Long on the last he dwelt, though every part
A pointed arrow sped to pierce his heart.
    Thus in a trice a judge of beauty grown,
(A judge erected from a country clown,)
He longed to see her eyes in slumber hid,
And wished his own could pierce within the lid.
He would have waked her, but restrained his thought,
And love new-born the first good manners taught.
An awful fear his ardent wish withstood,
Nor durst disturb the goddess of the wood;

For such she seemed by her celestial face,
Excelling all the rest of human race;
And things divine, by common sense he knew,
Must be devoutly seen at distant view:
So checking his desire, with trembling heart
Gazing he stood, nor would nor could depart;
Fixed as a pilgrim wildered in his way,
Who dares not stir by night, for fear to stray;
But stands with awful eyes to watch the dawn of day.

SIGISMONDA AND GUISCARDO

While Norman Tancred in Salerno reigned,
The title of a gracious prince he gained;
Till turned a tyrant in his latter days,
He lost the lustre of his former praise;
And from the bright meridian where he stood,
Descending, dipped his hands in lovers' blood.

This prince of fortune's favour long possessed,
Yet was with one fair daughter only blessed;
And blessed he might have been with her alone,
But oh! how much more happy, had he none!
She was his care, his hope, and his delight,
Most in his thought, and ever in his sight:
Next, nay beyond his life, he held her dear;
She lived by him, and now he lived in her.
For this, when ripe for marriage, he delayed
Her nuptial bonds, and kept her long a maid,
As envy any else should share a part
Of what was his, and claiming all her heart.
At length, as public decency required,
And all his vassals eagerly desired,
With mind averse, he rather underwent
His people's will, than gave his own consent.
So was she torn, as from a lover's side,
And made almost in his despite a bride.

Short were her marriage joys; for in the prime
Of youth, her lord expired before his time:
And to her father's court, in little space

Restored anew, she held a higher place;
More loved, and more exalted into grace.
This princess fresh and young, and fair, and wise,
The worshipped idol of her father's eyes,
Did all her sex in every grace exceed,
And had more wit beside than women need.
    Youth, health, and ease, and most an amorous
        mind,
To second nuptials had her thoughts inclined;
And former joys had left a secret sting behind.
But prodigal in every other grant,
Her sire left unsupplied her only want;
And she, betwixt her modesty and pride,
Her wishes, which she could not help, would hide.
    Resolved at last to lose no longer time,
And yet to please herself without a crime,
She cast her eyes around the court, to find
A worthy subject suiting to her mind,
To him in holy nuptials to be tied,
A seeming widow, and a secret bride.
Among the train of courtiers, one she found
With all the gifts of bounteous nature crowned,
Of gentle blood, but one whose niggard fate
Had set him far below her high estate:
Guiscard his name was called, of blooming age,
Now squire to Tancred, and before his page:
To him, the choice of all the shining crowd,
Her heart the noble Sigismonda vowed.
    Yet hitherto she kept her love concealed,

And with close glances every day beheld
The graceful youth; and every day increased
The raging fire that burned within her breast;
Some secret charm did all his acts attend,
And what his fortune wanted, hers could mend:
Till, as the fire will force its outward way,
Or, in the prison pent, consume the prey,
So long her earnest eyes on his were set,
At length their twisted rays together met;
And he, surprised with humble joy, surveyed
One sweet regard, shot by the royal maid.
Not well assured, while doubtful hopes he nursed,
A second glance came gliding like the first;
And he who saw the sharpness of the dart,
Without defence received it in his heart.
In public though their passion wanted speech,
Yet mutual looks interpreted for each:
Time, ways, and means of meeting were denied,
But all those wants ingenious love supplied.
The inventive god, who never fails his part,
Inspires the wit, when once he warms the heart.

When Guiscard next was in the circle seen,
Where Sigismonda held the place of queen,
A hollow cane within her hand she brought,
But in the concave had enclosed a note;
With this she seemed to play, and, as in sport,
Tossed to her love, in presence of the court;
'Take it,' she said; 'and when your needs require,
This little brand will serve to light your fire.'

He took it with a bow, and soon divined
The seeming toy was not for nought designed:
But when retired, so long with curious eyes
He viewed the present, that he found the prize.
Much was in little writ; and all conveyed
With cautious care, for fear to be betrayed
By some false confident, or favourite maid.
The time, the place, the manner how to meet,
Were all in punctual order plainly writ:
But since a trust must be, she thought it best
To put it out of laymen's power at least,
And for their solemn vows prepared a priest.

Guiscard (her secret purpose understood)
With joy prepared to meet the coming good;
Nor pains nor danger was resolved to spare,
But use the means appointed by the fair.

Near the proud palace of Salerno stood
A mount of rough ascent, and thick with wood,
Through this a cave was dug with vast expense,
The work it seemed of some suspicious prince,
Who, when abusing power with lawless might,
From public justice would secure his flight.
The passage made by many a winding way,
Reached e'en the room in which the tyrant lay,
Fit for his purpose; on a lower floor
He lodged, whose issue was an iron door,
From whence, by stairs descending to the ground,
In the blind grot a safe retreat he found.
Its outlet ended in a brake o'ergrown

With brambles, choked by time, and now unknown.
A rift there was, which from the mountain's height,
Conveyed a glimmering and malignant light,
A breathing-place to draw the damps away,
A twilight of an intercepted day.
The tyrant's den, whose use though lost to fame,
Was now the apartment of the royal dame;
The cavern only to her father known,
By him was to his darling daughter shown.

Neglected long she let the secret rest,
Till love recalled it to her labouring breast,
And hinted as the way by heaven designed
The teacher, by the means he taught, to blind.
What will not women do, when need inspires
Their wit, or love their inclination fires!
Though jealousy of state the invention found,
Yet love refined upon the former ground.
That way the tyrant had reserved to fly
Pursuing hate, now served to bring two lovers nigh.

The dame, who long in vain had kept the key,
Bold by desire, explored the secret way;
Now tried the stairs, and wading through the night,
Searched all the deep recess, and issued into light.
All this her letter had so well explained,
The instructed youth might compass what remained:
The cavern-mouth alone was hard to find,
Because the path disused was out of mind:
But in what quarter of the copse it lay,
His eye by certain level could survey:

Yet (for the wood perplexed with thorns he knew)
A frock of leather o'er his limbs he drew:
And thus provided, searched the brake around,
Till the choked entry of the cave he found.

  Thus, all prepared, the promised hour arrived,
So long expected, and so well contrived:
With love to friend, the impatient lover went,
Fenced from the thorns, and trod the deep descent.
The conscious priest, who was suborned before,
Stood ready posted at the postern door;
The maids in distant rooms were sent to rest,
And nothing wanted but the invited guest.
He came, and knocking thrice, without delay,
The longing lady heard, and turned the key;
At once invaded him with all her charms,
And the first step he made, was in her arms:
The leathern outside, boistrous as it was,
Gave way, and bent beneath her strict embrace:
On either side the kisses flew so thick,
That neither he nor she had breath to speak.
The holy man amazed at what he saw,
Made haste to sanctify the bliss by law;
And muttered fast the matrimony o'er,
For fear committed sin should get before.
His work performed, he left the pair alone,
Because he knew he could not go too soon;
His presence odious, when his task was done.
What thoughts he had, beseems not me to say,
Though some surmise he went to fast and pray,

And needed both, to drive the tempting thoughts away.

  The foe once gone, they took their full delight;
'Twas restless rage, and tempest all the night:
For greedy love each moment would employ,
And grudged the shortest pauses of their joy.

  Thus were their loves auspiciously begun,
And thus with secret care were carried on.
The stealth itself did appetite restore,
And looked so like a sin, it pleased the more.

  The cave was now become a common way,
The wicket often opened, knew the key.
Love rioted secure, and long enjoyed,
Was ever eager, and was never cloyed.

  But as extremes are short, of ill and good,
And tides at highest mark regorge the flood;
So fate, that could no more improve their joy,
Took a malicious pleasure to destroy.

  Tancred, who fondly loved, and whose delight
Was placed in his fair daughter's daily sight,
Of custom, when his state affairs were done,
Would pass his pleasing hours with her alone:
And, as a father's privilege allowed,
Without attendance of the officious crowd.

  It happened once, that when in heat of day
He tried to sleep, as was his usual way,
The balmy slumber fled his wakeful eyes,
And forced him, in his own despite, to rise:
Of sleep forsaken, to relieve his care,
  He sought the conversation of the fair:

But with her train of damsels she was gone,
In shady walks the scorching heat to shun:
He would not violate that sweet recess,
And found besides a welcome heaviness
That seized his eyes; and slumber, which forgot
When called before to come, now came unsought.
From light retired, behind his daughter's bed,
He for approaching sleep composed his head;
A chair was ready, for that use designed,
So quilted, that he lay at ease reclined;
The curtains closely drawn, the light to screen,
As if he had contrived to lie unseen:
Thus covered with an artificial night,
Sleep did his office soon, and sealed his sight.
    With heaven averse, in this ill-omened hour
Was Guiscard summoned to the secret bower,
And the fair nymph, with expectation fired,
From her attending damsels was retired:
For, true to love, she measured time so right,
As not to miss one moment of delight.
The garden, seated on the level floor,
She left behind, and locking every door,
Thought all secure; but little did she know,
Blind to her fate, she had enclosed her foe.
Attending Guiscard, in his leathern frock,
Stood ready, with his thrice-repeated knock:
Thrice with a doleful sound the jarring grate
Rung deaf, and hollow, and presaged their fate.
The door unlocked, to known delight they haste,

And panting in each other's arms, embraced;
Rush to the conscious bed, a mutual freight.
And heedless press it with their wonted weight.

The sudden bound awaked the sleeping sire,
And showed a sight no parent can desire:
His opening eyes at once with odious view
The love discovered, and the lover knew:
He would have cried; but hoping that he dreamt,
Amazement tied his tongue, and stopped the attempt.
The ensuing moment all the truth declared,
But now he stood collected, and prepared;
For malice and revenge had put him on his guard.

So, like a lion that unheeded lay,
Dissembling sleep, and watchful to betray,
With inward rage he meditates his prey.
The thoughtless pair, indulging their desires,
Alternate kindled and then quenched their fires;
Nor thinking in the shades of death they played,
Full of themselves, themselves alone surveyed,
And, too secure, were by themselves betrayed.
Long time dissolved in pleasure thus they lay,
Till nature could no more suffice their play;
Then rose the youth, and through the cave again
Returned; the princess mingled with her train.

Resolved his unripe vengeance to defer,
The royal spy, when now the coast was clear,
Sought not the garden, but retired unseen,
To brood in secret on his gathered spleen,
And methodize revenge: to death he grieved;

And, but he saw the crime, had scarce believed.
The appointment for the ensuing night he heard;
And therefore in the cavern had prepared
Two brawny yeomen of his trusty guard.

 Scarce had unwary Guiscard set his foot
Within the farmost entrance of the grot,
When these in secret ambush ready lay,
And rushing on the sudden seized the prey:
Encumbered with his frock, without defence,
An easy prize, they led the prisoner thence,
And, as commanded, brought before the prince.
The gloomy sire, too sensible of wrong
To vent his rage in words, restrained his tongue;
And only said, 'Thus servants are preferred,
And trusted, thus their sovereigns they reward.
Had I not seen, had not these eyes received
So clear a proof, I could not have believed.'

 He paused, and choked the rest. The youth who saw
His forfeit life abandoned to the law,
The judge the accuser, and the offence to him
Who had both power and will to avenge the crime,
No vain defence prepared; but thus replied,
'The faults of love by love are justified:
With unresisted might the monarch reigns,
He levels mountains, and he raises plains;
And not regarding difference of degree,
Abased your daughter, and exalted me.'

 This bold return with seeming patience heard,
The prisoner was remitted to the guard.

The sullen tyrant slept not all the night,
But lonely walking by a winking light,
Sobbed, wept, and groaned, and beat his withered
   breast,
But would not violate his daughter's rest;
Who long expecting lay, for bliss prepared,
Listening for noise, and grieved that none she heard;
Oft rose, and oft in vain employed the key,
And oft accused her lover of delay;
And passed the tedious hours in anxious thoughts
   away.
   The morrow came; and at his usual hour
Old Tancred visited his daughter's bower;
Her cheek (for such his custom was) he kissed,
Then blessed her kneeling, and her maids dismissed.
The royal dignity thus far maintained,
Now left in private, he no longer feigned,
But all at once his grief and rage appeared,
And floods of tears ran trickling down his beard.
   'O Sigismonda,' he began to say:
Thrice he began, and thrice was forced to stay,
Till words with often trying found their way:
'I thought, O Sigismonda, (but how blind
Are parents' eyes, their children's faults to find!)
Thy virtue, birth, and breeding were above
A mean desire, and vulgar sense of love:
Nor less than sight and hearing could convince
So fond a father, and so just a prince,
Of such an unforeseen, and unbelieved offence.

74

Then what indignant sorrow must I have,
To see thee lie subjected to my slave!
A man so smelling of the people's lee,
The court received him first for charity;
And since with no degree of honour graced,
But only suffered, where he first was placed:
A grovelling insect still; and so designed
By nature's hand, nor born of noble kind:
A thing, by neither man nor woman prized,
And scarcely known enough, to be despised.
To what has heaven reserved my age? Ah why
Should man, when nature calls, not choose to die,
Rather than stretch the span of life, to find
Such ills as fate has wisely cast behind,
For those to feel, whom fond desire to live
Makes covetous of more than life can give!
Each has his share of good, and when 'tis gone,
The guest, though hungry, cannot rise too soon.
But I, expecting more, in my own wrong
Protracting life, have lived a day too long.
If yesterday could be recalled again,
E'en now would I conclude my happy reign:
But 'tis too late, my glorious race is run.
Hadst thou not loved, or loving saved the shame,
If not the sin, by some illustrious name,
This little comfort had relieved my mind,
'Twas fraility, not unusual to thy kind:
But thy low fall beneath the royal blood,
Shows downward appetite to mix with mud:

Thus not the least excuse is left for thee,
Nor the least refuge for unhappy me.

   'For him I have resolved: whom by surprise
I took, and scarce can call it, in disguise;
For such was his attire, as with intent
Of nature, suited to his mean descent:
The harder question yet remains behind,
What pains a parent and a price can find
To punish an offence of this degenerate kind.

   'As I have loved, and yet I love thee more
Than ever father loved a child before;
So that indulgence draws me to forgive:
Nature, that gave thee life, would have thee live.
But, as a public parent of the state,
My justice, and thy crime, require thy fate.
Fain would I choose a middle course to steer;
Nature's too kind, and justice too severe:
Speak for us both, and to the balance bring
On either side, the father, and the king.
Heaven knows, my heart is bent to favour thee;
Make it but scanty weight, and leave the rest to me.'

   Here stopping with a sigh, he poured a flood
Of tears, to make his last expression good.

   She, who had heard him speak, nor saw alone
The secret conduct of her love was known,
But he was taken who her soul possessed,
Felt all the pangs of sorrows in her breast;
And little wanted, but a woman's heart
With cries, and tears, had testified her smart:

But inborn worth, that fortune can control,
New strung, and stiffer bent her softer soul;
The heroine assumed the woman's place,
Confirmed her mind, and fortified her face:
Why should she beg, or what could she pretend,
When her stern father had condemned her friend!
Her life she might have had; but her despair
Of saving his, had put it past her care:
Resolved on fate, she would not lose her breath,
But rather than not die, solicit death.
Fixed on this thought, she, not as women use
Her fault by common frailty would excuse,
But boldly justified her innocence,
And while the fact was owned, denied the offence:
Then with dry eyes, and with an open look,
She met his glance midway, and thus undaunted
    spoke.

'Tancred, I neither am disposed to make
Request for life nor offered life to take:
Much less deny the deed; but least of all
Beneath pretended justice weakly fall.
My words to sacred truth shall be confined,
My deeds shall show the greatness of my mind.
That I have loved, I own; that still I love,
I call to witness all the powers above:
Yet more I own: to Guiscard's love I give
The small remaining time I have to live;
And if beyond this life desire can be,
Not fate itself shall set my passion free.

'This first avowed; nor folly warped my mind,
Nor the frail texture of the female kind
Betrayed my virtue: for, too well I knew
What honour was, and honour had his due:
Before the holy priest my vows were tied,
So came I not a strumpet, but a bride;
This for my fame: and for the public voice:
Yet more, his merits justified my choice;
Which had they not, the first election thine,
That bond dissolved, the next is freely mine:
Or grant I erred, (which yet I must deny)
Had parents power e'en second vows to tie,
Thy little care to mend my widowed nights
Has forced me to recourse of marriage rites,
To fill an empty side, and follow known delights.
What have I done in this, deserving blame?
State laws may alter: nature's are the same;
Those are usurped on helpless woman-kind,
Made without our consent, and wanting power to
    bind.

'Thou, Tancred, better shouldst have understood,
That as thy father gave thee flesh and blood,
So gavest thou me: not from the quarry hewed,
But of a softer mould, with sense endued;
E'en softer than thy own, of suppler kind,
More exquisite of taste, and more than man refined.
Nor needst thou by thy daughter to be told,
Though now thy sprightly blood with age be cold,
Thou hast been young; and canst remember still,

That when thou hadst the power, thou hadst the will;
And from the past experience of thy fires,
Canst tell with what a tide our strong desires
Come rushing on in youth, and what their rage
   requires.
   'And grant thy youth was exercised in arms,
When love no leisure found for softer charms,
My tender age in luxury was trained,
With idle ease and pageants entertained;
My hours my own, my pleasures unrestrained.
So bred, no wonder if I took the bent
That seemed e'en warrented by thy consent;
For, when the father is too fondly kind,
Such seed he sows, such harvest shall he find.
Blame then thyself, as reason's law requires,
(Since nature gave, and thou fomentst my fires;)
If still those appetites continue strong,
Thou mayst consider, I am yet but young:
Consider too, that having been a wife,
I must have tasted of a better life,
And am not to be blamed, if I renew,
By lawful means, the joys which then I knew.
Where was the crime, if pleasure I procured,
Young, and a woman, and to bliss inured?
That was my case, and this is my defence:
I pleased myself, I shunned incontinence,
And urged by strong desires, indulged my sense.
   'Left to myself, I must avow, I strove
From public shame to screen my secret love,

And well acquainted with thy native pride,
Endeavoured, what I could not help, to hide;
For which, a woman's wit an easy way supplied.
How this, so well contrived, so closely laid,
Was known to thee, or by what chance betrayed,
Is not my care: to please thy pride alone,
I could have wished it had been still unknown.

   'Nor took I Guiscard by blind fancy led,
Or hasty choice, as many women wed;
But with deliberate care, and ripened thought,
At leisure first designed, before I wrought:
On him I rested, after long debate,
And not without considering, fixed my fate:
His flame was equal, though by mine inspired;
(For so the difference of our birth required:)
Had he been born like me, like me his love
Had first begun what mine was forced to move:
But thus beginning, thus we persevere;
Our passions yet continue what they were,
Nor length of trial makes our joys the less sincere.

   'At this my choice, though not by thine allowed,
(Thy judgment herding with the common crowd)
Thou takest unjust offence; and, led by them
Dost less the merit than the man esteem.
Too sharply, Tancred, by thy pride betrayed,
Hast thou against the laws of kind inveighed;
For all the offence is in opinion placed,
Which deems high birth by lowly choice debased:
This thought alone with fury fires thy breast,

(For holy marriage justifies the rest)
That I have sunk the glories of the state,
And mixed my blood with a plebeian mate:
In which I wonder thou shouldst oversee
Superior causes, or impute to me
The fault of fortune, or the fates' decree.
Or call it heaven's imperial power alone,
Which moves on springs of justice, though unknown;
Yet this we see, though ordered for the best,
The bad exalted, and the good oppressed;
Permitted laurels grace the lawless brow,
The unworthy raised, the worthy cast below.
  'But leaving that: search we the secret springs,
And backward trace the principles of things;
There shall we find, that when the world began,
One common mass composed the mould of man;
One paste of flesh on all degrees bestowed,
And kneaded up alike with moistening blood.
The same almighty power inspired the frame
With kindled life, and formed the souls the same:
The faculties of intellect, and will,
Dispensed with equal hand, disposed with equal skill,
Like liberty indulged with choice of good or ill.
Thus born alike, from virtue first began
The difference that distinguished man from man:
He claimed no title from descent of blood,
But that which made him noble made him good:
Warmed with more particles of heavenly flame;
He winged his upward flight, and soared to fame;

The rest remained below, a tribe without a name.

'This law, though custom now diverts the course,
As nature's institute, is yet in force;
Uncancelled, though disused: and he whose mind
Is virtuous, is alone of noble kind.
Though poor in fortune, of celestial race;
And he commits the crime, who calls him base.

'Now lay the line; and measure all thy court,
By inward virtue, not external port,
And find whom justly to prefer above
The man on whom my judgment placed my love:
So shalt thou see his parts, and person shine;
And thus compared, the rest a base degenerate line.
Nor took I, when I first surveyed thy court,
His valour, or his virtues on report;
But trusted what I ought to trust alone,
Relying on thy eyes, and not my own;
Thy praise (and thine was then the public voice)
First recommended Guiscard to my choice:
Directed thus by thee, I looked and found
A man I thought deserving to be crowned;
First by my father pointed to my sight,
Nor less conspicuous by his native light:
His mind, his mien, the features of his face,
Excelling all the rest of human race:
These were thy thoughts, and thou couldst judge
    aright,
Till interest made a jaundice in thy sight.

'Or should I grant, thou didst not rightly see;

Then thou wert first deceived, and I deceived by thee.
But if thou shalt allege, through pride of mind,
Thy blood with one of base condition joined,
'Tis false; for 'tis not baseness to be poor;
His poverty augments thy crime the more;
Upbraids thy justice with the scant regard
Of worth: whom princes praise, they should reward.
Are these the kings entrusted by the crowd
With wealth to be dispensed for common good?
The people sweat not for their king's delight,
To enrich a pimp, or raise a parasite;
Theirs is the toil; and he who well has served
His country, has his country's wealth deserved.

 'E'en might monarchs oft are meanly born,
And kings by birth, to lowest rank return;
All subject to the power of giddy chance,
For fortune can depress, or can advance:
But true nobility is of the mind,
Not given by chance, and not to chance resigned.

 'For the remaining doubt of thy decree,
What to resolve, and how dispose of me,
Be warned to cast that useless care aside,
My self alone, will for myself provide:
If in thy doting, and decrepit age,
Thy soul, a stranger in the youth to rage,
Begins in cruel deeds to take delight,
Gorge with my blood thy barbarous appetite;
For I so little am disposed to pray
For life, I would not cast a wish away.

Such as it is, the offence is all my own;
And what to Guiscard is already done,
Or to be done, is doomed by thy decree,
That, if not executed first by thee,
Shall on my person be performed by me.

'Away! with women weep, and leave me here,
Fixed, like a man to die, without a tear;
Or save, or slay us both this present hour,
'Tis all that fate has left within thy power.'

She said; nor did her father fail to find,
In all she spoke, the greatness of her mind;
Yet thought she was not obstinate to die,
Nor deemed the death she promised was so nigh:
Secure in this belief, he left the dame,
Resolved to spare her life, and save her shame;
But that detested object to remove,
To wreak his vengeance, and to cure her love.

Intent on this, a secret order signed,
The death of Guiscard to his guards enjoined:
Strangling was chosen, and the night the time,
A mute revenge, and blind as was the crime:
His faithful heart, a bloody sacrifice,
Torn from his breast, to glut the tyrant's eyes,
Closed the severe command: for, (slaves to pay)
What kings decree, the soldier must obey:
Waged against foes; and, when the wars are o'er
Fit only to maintain despotic power:
Dangerous to freedom, and desired alone
By kings, who seek an arbitrary throne:

Such were these guards; as ready to have slain
The prince himself, allured with greater gain:
So was the charge performed with better will,
By men enured to blood, and exercised in ill.

Now, though the sullen sire had eased his mind,
The pomp of his revenge was yet behind,
A pomp prepared to grace the present he designed.
A goblet rich with gems, and rough with gold,
Of depth, and breadth, the precious pledge to hold,
With cruel care he chose: the hollow part
Enclosed; the lid concealed the lover's heart:
Then of his trusted mischiefs, one he sent,
And bade him with these words the gift present:
'Thy father sends thee this, to cheer thy breast,
And glad thy sight with what thou lovest the best;
As thou hast pleased his eyes, and joyed his mind,
With what he loved the most of human kind.'

Ere this the royal dame, who well had weighed
The consequence of what her sire had said,
Fixed on her fate, against the expected hour,
Procured the means to have it in her power:
For this, she had distilled, with early care,
The juice of simples, friendly to despair,
A magazine of death; and thus prepared,
Secure to die, the fatal message heard:
Then smiled severe; nor with a troubled look,
Or trembling hand, the funeral present took;
E'en kept her countenance, when the lid removed,
Disclosed the heart unfortunately loved:

She needed not be told within whose breast
It lodged; the message had explained the rest.
Or not amazed, or hiding her surprise,
She sternly on the bearer fixed her eyes:
Then thus: 'Tell Tancred on his daughter's part,
The gold, though precious, equals not the heart:
But he did well to give his best; and I,
Who wished a worthier urn, forgive his poverty.'

At this, she curbed a groan, that else had come,
And pausing, viewed the present in the tomb:
Then to the heart adored devoutly glued
Her lips, and raising it, her speech renewed:
'E'en from my day of birth, to this, the bound
Of my unhappy being, I have found
My father's care and tenderness expressed.
But this last act of love excels the rest:
For this so dear a present, bear him back
The best return that I can live to make.'

*   *   *

The messenger dispatched, again she viewed
The loved remains and, sighing, thus pursued:
'Source of my life, and lord of my desires,
In whom I lived, with whom my soul expires;
Poor heart, no more the spring of vital heat,
Cursed be the hands that tore thee from thy seat!
The course is finished, which thy fates decreed,
And thou, from thy corporeal prison freed:
Soon hast thou reached the goal with mended
    pace,

A world of woes dispatched in little space:
Forced by the worth, thy foe in death become
Thy friend, has lodged thee in a costly tomb;
There yet remained thy funeral exequies,
The weeping tribute of thy widow's eyes,
And those, indulgent heaven has found the way
That I, before my death, have leave to pay.
My father e'en in cruelty is kind,
Or heaven has turned the malice of his mind
To better uses that his hate designed;
And made the insult which in his gift appears,
The means to mourn thee with my pious tears;
Which I will pay thee down, before I go,
And save myself the pains to weep below,
If souls can weep; thought once I meant to meet
My fate with face unmoved, and eyes unwet,
Yet since I have thee here in narrow room,
My tears shall set thee first afloat within thy tomb:
Then (as I know thy spirit hovers nigh)
Under thy friendly conduct will I fly
To regions unexplored, secure to share
Thy state; nor hell shall punishment appear,
And heaven is double heaven, if thou art there.'
  She said. Her brimful eyes, that ready stood,
And only wanted will to weep a flood,
Released their watery store, and poured amain,
Like clouds low hung, a sober shower of rain;
Mute solemn sorrow, free from female noise,
Such as the majesty of grief destroys:

For, bending o'er the cup, the tears she shed
Seemed by the posture to discharge her head,
O'erfilled before; and oft (her mouth applied
To the cold heart) she kissed at once and cried.
Her maids, who stood amazed, nor knew the cause
Of her complaining, nor whose heart it was;
Yet all due measures of her mourning kept,
Did office at the dirge, and by infection wept;
And oft inquired the occasion of her grief,
(Unanswered but by sighs) and offered vain relief.
At length, her stock of tears already shed,
She wiped her eyes, she raised her drooping head,
And thus pursued: 'O ever faithful heart,
I have performed the ceremonial part,
The decencies of grief. It rests behind,
That as our bodies were, our souls be joined:
To thy whate'er abode, my shade convey,
And as an elder ghost, direct the way.'
She said; and bade the vial to be brought,
Where she before had brewed the deadly draught,
First pouring out the medicinable bane,
The heart, her tears had rinsed, she bathed again;
Then down her throat the death securely throws,
And quaffs a long oblivion of her woes.

This done, she mounts the genial bed, and there,
(Her body first composed with honest care,)
Attends the welcome rest. Her hands yet hold
Close to her heart, the monumental gold;
Nor further word she spoke, but closed her sight,

And quiet, sought the covert of the night.

    The damsels, who the while in silence mourned,
Not knowing, nor suspecting death suborned,
Yet, and their duty was, to Tancred sent,
Who, conscious of the occasion, feared the event.
Alarmed, and with presaging heart he came,
And drew the curtains, and exposed the dame
To loathsome light: then with a late relief
Made vain efforts to mitigate her grief.
She, what she could excluding day, her eyes
Kept firmly sealed, and sternly thus replies:

    'Tancred, restrain thy tears, unsought by me,
And sorrow, unavailing now to thee:
Did ever man before afflict his mind
To see the effect of what himself designed?
Yet, if thou hast remaining in thy heart
Some sense of love, some unextinguished part
Of former kindness, largely once professed,
Let me by that adjure thy hardened breast,
Not to deny thy daughter's last request:
The secret love, which I so long enjoyed,
And still concealed, to gratify thy pride,
Thou hast disjoined; but with my dying breath,
Seek not, I beg thee, to disjoin our death:
Where'er his corpse by thy command is laid,
Thither let mine in public be conveyed;
Exposed in open view, and side by side,
Acknowledged as a bridegroom and a bride.'

    The prince's anguish hindered his reply;

And she, who felt her fate approaching nigh,
Seized the cold heart, and heaving to her breast,
'Here, precious pledge,' she said, 'securely rest.'
These accents were her last; the creeping death
Benumbed her senses first, then stopped her breath.

Thus she for disobedience justly died;
The sire was justly punished for his pride:
The youth, least guilty, suffered for the offence
Of duty violated to his prince;
Who late repenting of his cruel deed,
One common sepulchre for both decreed;
Entombed the wretched pair in royal state,
And on their monument inscribed their fate.

SONG

Ah fading joy, how quickly art thou past?
  Yet we thy ruine haste:
As if the cares of Humane Life were few
  We seek out new:
And follow Fate that does too fast pursue.

See how on every bough the Birds express
  In the sweet notes their happiness.
 They all enjoy, and nothing spare;
 But on their Mother Nature lay their care:
Why then should Man, the Lord of all below
  Such troubles chuse to know
As none of all his Subjects undergo?

 Hark, hark, the Waters fall, fall, fall;
 And with a Murmuring sound
 Dash, dash, upon the ground,
  To gentle slumbers call.

SONG

Ah how sweet it is to love,
Ah how gay is young desire!
And what pleasing pains we prove
When we first approach Loves fire!
   Pains of Love be sweeter far
   Than all other pleasures are.

Sighs which are from Lovers blown,
Do but gently heave the Heart;
Ev'n the tears they shed alone
Cure, like trickling Balm their smart.
   Lovers when they lose their breath,
   Bleed away in easie death.

Love and Time with reverence use,
Treat 'em like a parting friend:
Nor the golden gifts refuse
Which in youth sincere they send:
   For each year their price is more,
   And they less simple than before.

Love, like Spring-tides full and high,
Swells in every youthful vein:
But each Tide does less supply,
Till they quite shrink in again:
   If a flow in Age appear,
   'Tis but rain, and runs not clear.

SONG

You charm'd me not with that fair face
   Though it was all divine:
To be anothers is the Grace,
   That makes me wish you mine.
The Gods and Fortune take their part
   Who like young Monarchs fight;
And boldly dare invade that heart
   Which is anothers right.
First mad with hope we undertake
   To pull up every barr;
But once possess'd, we faintly make
   A dull defensive warr.
Now every friend is turn'd a foe
   In hope to get our store:
And passion makes us Cowards grow,
   Which made us brave before.

SONG

Why should a foolish Marriage Vow
   Which long ago was made,
Oblige us to each other now
   When Passion is decay'd?
We lov'd, and we lov'd, as long as we cou'd,
   Till our love was lov'd out in us both:
But our Marriage is dead, when the Pleasure is fled
   'Twas Pleasure first made it an Oath.

If I have Pleasures for a Friend,
   And farther love in store,
What wrong has he whose joys did end,
   And who cou'd give no more?

'Tis a madness that he
Should be jealous of me,
Or that I shou'd bar him of another:
For all we can gain,
Is to give our selves pain,
When neither can hinder the other.

earning flourished, only knew,

ı this day renew.

ıl rites to Pallas done,

ıes lost or won.

crowned with olives, sit,

red horror from the pit.

A day, ɔm is this of your decree,
Where e'en the best are but by mercy free;
A day, which none but Jonson durst have wished to
see.
Here they, who long have known the useful stage,
Come to be taught themselves to teach the age.
As your commissioners our poets go,
To cultivate the virtue which you sow;
In your Lyceum first themselves refined,
And delegated thence to humankind.
But as ambassadors, when long from home,
For new instructions to their princes come,
So poets, who your precepts have forgot,
Return, and beg they may be better taught:
Follies and faults elsewhere by them are shown,
But by your manners they correct their own.
The illiterate writer, emp'ric-like, applies
To minds diseased, unsafe chance remedies:
The learned in schools, where knowledge first began,
Studies with care the anatomy of man;
See virtue, vice, and passions in their cause,

And fame from science, not from fortune, draws;
So poetry, which is in Oxford made
An art, in London only is a trade.
There haughty dunces, whose unlearned pen
Could ne'er spell grammar, would be reading men.
Such build their poems the Lucretian way;
So many huddled atoms make a play;
And if they hit in order by some chance,
They call that nature, which is ignorance.
To such a fame let mere town-wits aspire,
And their gay nonsense their own cits admire.
Out poet, could he find forgiveness here,
Would wish it rather than a plaudit there.
He owns no crown from those Praetorian bands,
But knows *that* right is in this senate's hands.
Not impudent enough to hope your praise,
Low at the muses' feet his wreath he lays,
And, where he took it up, resigns his bays.
Kings make their poets whom themselves think fit,
But 'tis your suffrage makes authentic wit.

EPILOGUE TO OXFORD

Oft has our poet wished this happy seat
Might prove his fading muse's last retreat:
I wondered at his wish, but now I find
He sought for quiet, and content of mind;
Which noiseful towns, and courts, can never know,
And only in the shades like laurels grow.
Youth, ere it sees the world, here studies rest,
And age returning thence concludes it best.
What wonder if we court that happiness
Yearly to share, which hourly you possess,
Teaching e'en you, while the vexed world we show,
Your peace to value more, and better know?
'Tis all we can return for favours past,
Whose holy memory shall ever last,
For patronage from him whose care presides
O'er every noble art, and every science guides:
Bathurst, a name the learned with reverence know,
And scarcely more to his own Virgil owe;
Whose age enjoys but what his youth deserved,
To rule those muses whom before he served.
His learning, and untainted manners too,
We find, Athenians, are derived to you:
Such ancient hospitality there rests
In yours, as dwelt in the first Grecian breasts,
Whose kindness was religion to their guests.
Such modesty did to our sex appear,
As, had there been no laws, we need not fear,

Since each of you was our protector here.
Converse so chaste, and so strict virtue shown,
As might Apollo with the muses own.
Till our return, we must despair to find
Judges so just, so knowing, and so kind.

CONCERNING THE NATURE OF LOVE

Thus therefore, he who feels the fiery dart
Of strong desire transfix his amorous heart,
Whether some beauteous boy's alluring face,
Or lovelier maid, with unresisting grace,
From her each part the winged arrow sends,
From whence he first was struck he thither tends;
Restless he roams, impatient to be freed,
And eager to inject the sprightly seed;
For fierce desire does all his mind employ,
And ardent love assures approaching joy.
Such is the nature of that pleasing smart,
Whose burning drops distil upon the heart,
The fever of the soul shot from the fair,
And the cold ague of succeeding care.
If absent, her idea still appears,
And her sweet name is chiming in your ears.
But strive those pleasing phantoms to remove,
And shun the aerial images of love
That feed the flame: when one molests thy mind,
Discharge thy loins on all the leaky kind;
For that's a wiser way, than to restrain
Within thy swelling nerves that hoard of pain
For every hour some deadlier symptom shows,
And by delay the gathering venom grows,
When kindly applications are not used;
The scorpion, love, must on the wound be bruised.
On that one object 'tis not safe to stay,

But force the tide of thought some other way;
The squandered spirits prodigally throw,
And in the common glebe of nature sow.
Nor wants he all the bliss that lovers feign,
Who takes the pleasure, and avoids the pain;
For purer joys in purer health abound,
And less affect the sickly than the sound.

When love its utmost vigour does employ,
E'en then 'tis but a restless wandering joy;
Nor knows the lover in that wild excess,
With hands or eyes, what first he would possess:
But strains at all, and fastening where he strains,
Too closely presses with his frantic pains;
With biting kisses hurts the twining fair,
Which shows his joys imperfect, insincere:
For, stung with inward rage, he flings around,
And strives to avenge the smart on that which gave
     the wound.
But love those eager bitings does restrain,
And mingling pleasure mollifies the pain.
For ardent hope still flatters anxious grief,
And sends him to his foe to seek relief:
Which yet the nature of the thing denies;
For love, and love alone of all our joys,
By full possession does but fan the fire;
The more we still enjoy, the more we still desire.
Nature for meat and drink provides a space,
And when received, they fill their certain place;
Hence thirst and hunger may be satisfied,

But this repletion is to love denied:
Form, feature, colour, whatsoe'er delight
Provokes the lover's endless appetite,
These fill no space, nor can we thence remove
With lips, or hands, or all our instruments of love:
In our deluded grasp we nothing find,
But thin aerial shapes, that fleet before the mind.
As he, who in a dream with drought is cursed,
And finds no real drink to quench his thirst,
Runs to imagined lakes his heat to steep,
And vainly swills and labours in his sleep;
So love with phantoms cheats our longing eyes,
Which hourly seeing never satisfies:
Our hands pull nothing from the parts they strain,
But wander o'er the lovely limbs in vain.
Nor when the youthful pair more closely join,
When hands in hands they lock, and thighs in thighs
    they twine,
Just in the raging foam of full desire,
When both press on, both murmur, both expire,
They grip, they squeeze, their humid tongues they
    dart,
As each would force their way to t'other's heart:
In vain; they only cruise about the coast;
For bodies cannot pierce, nor be in bodies lost,
As sure they strive to be, when both engage
In that tumultuous momentary rage;
So tangled in the nets of love they lie,
Till man dissolves in that excess of joy.

Then, when the gathered bag has burst its way,
And ebbing tides the slackened nerves betray,
A pause ensues; and nature nods awhile,
Till with recruited rage new spirits boil;
And then the same vain violence returns,
With flames renewed the erected furnace burns;
Again they in each other would be lost,
But still by adamantine bars are crossed.
All ways they try, successless all they prove,
To cure the secret sore of lingering love.
  Besides –
They waste their strength in the venereal strife,
And to a woman's will enslave their life;
The estate runs out, and mortgages are made,
All offices of friendship are decayed,
Their fortune ruined, and their fame betrayed.
Assyrian ointment from their temples flows,
And diamond buckles sparkle at their shoes;
The cheerful emerald twinkles on their hands,
With all the luxury of foreign lands;
And the blue coat, that with embroidery shines,
Is drunk with sweat of their o'er-laboured loins.
Their frugal father's gains they misemploy,
And turn to point, and pearl, and every female toy.
French fashions, costly treats are their delight;
The park by day, and plays and balls by night.
In vain; –
For in the fountain, where their sweets are sought,
Some bitter bubbles up, and poisons all the draught.

First, guilty conscience does the mirror bring,
Then sharp remorse shoots out her angry sting;
And anxious thoughts, within themselves at strife,
Upbraid the long misspent, luxurious life.
Perhaps the fickle fair one proves unkind,
Or drops a doubtful word, that pains his mind,
And leaves a rankling jealousy behind.
Perhaps he watches close her amorous eyes,
And in the act of ogling does surprise,
And thinks he sees upon her cheeks the while
The dimpled tracks of some foregoing smile;
His raging pulse beats thick, and his pent spirits boil.
This is the product e'en of prosperous love;
Think then what pangs disastrous passions prove;
Innumerable ills; disdain, despair,
With all the meagre family of care.

   Thus, as I said, 'tis better to prevent,
Than flatter the disease, and late repent;
Because to shun the allurement is not hard
To minds resolved, forewarned, and well prepared;
But wondrous difficult, when once beset,
To struggle through the straits, and break the
    involving net.

   Yet thus ensnared thy freedom thou may'st gain,
If, like a fool, thou dost not hug thy chain;
If not to ruin obstinately blind,
And wilfully endeavouring not to find
Her plain defects of body and of mind.
For thus the bedlam train of lovers use

To enhance the value, and the faults excuse;
And therefore 'tis no wonder if we see
They dote on dowdies and deformity.
E'en what they cannot praise, they will not blame,
But veil with some extenuating name.
The sallow skin is for the swarthy put,
And love can make a slattern of a slut;
If cat-eyed, then a Pallas is their love;
If freckled, she's a particoloured dove;
If little, then she's life and soul all o'er;
An Amazon, the large two-handed whore.
She stammers; oh, what grace in lisping lies!
If she says nothing, to be sure she's wise.
If shrill, and with a voice to drown a choir,
Sharp-witted she must be, and full of fire;
The lean, consumptive wench, with coughs decayed,
Is called a pretty, tight, and slender maid;
The o'ergrown, a goodly Ceres is expressed,
A bed-fellow for Bacchus at the least;
Flat-nose the name of Satyr never misses,
And hanging blubber lips but pout for kisses.
The task were endless all the rest to trace;
Yet grant she were a Venus for her face
And shape, yet others equal beauty share,
And time was you could live without the fair;
She does no more, in that for which you woo,
Than homelier women full as well can do.
Besides, she daubs, and stinks so much of paint,
Her own attendants cannot bear the scent,

But laugh behind, and bite their lips to hold.
Meantime excluded, and exposed to cold,
The whining lover stands before the gates,
And there with humble adoration waits;
Crowning with flowers the threshold and the floor,
And printing kisses on the obdurate door;
Who, if admitted in that nick of time,
If some unsavoury whiff betray the crime,
Invents a quarrel straight, if there be none,
Or makes some faint excuses to be gone;
And calls himself a doting fool to serve,
Ascribing more than woman can deserve;
Which well they understand, like cunning queans,
And hide their nastiness behind the scenes,
From him they have allured, and would retain;
But to a piercing eye 'tis all in vain:
For common sense brings all their cheats to view,
And the false light discovers by the true;
Which a wise harlot owns, and hopes to find
A pardon for defects, that run through all the kind.
  Nor always do they feign the sweets of love,
When round the panting youth their pliant limbs they
    move,
And cling, and heave, and moisten every kiss;
They often share, and more than share the bliss:
From every part, e'en to their inmost soul,
They feel the trickling joys, and run with vigour to the
    goal.
Stirred with the same impetuous desire,

Birds, beasts, and herds, and mares, their males
   require;
Because the throbbing nature in their veins
Provokes them to assuage their kindly pains.
The lusty leap the expecting female stands,
By mutual heat compelled to mutual bands.
Thus dogs with lolling tongues by love are tied,
Nor shouting boys nor blows their union can divide;
At either end they strive the link to loose,
In vain, for stronger Venus holds the noose;
Which never would those wretched lovers do,
But that the common heats of love they know;
The pleasure therefore must be shared in common too:
And when the woman's more prevailing juice
Sucks in the man's, the mixture will produce,
The mother's likeness; when the man prevails,
His own resemblance in the seed he seals.
But when we see the new-begotten race
Reflect the features of each parent's face,
Then of the father's and the mother's blood
The justly tempered seed is understood;
When both conspire, with equal ardour bent,
From every limb the due proportion sent,
When neither party foils, when neither foiled,
This gives the blended features of the child.
Sometimes the boy the grandsire's image bears;
Sometimes the more remote progenitor he shares;
Because the genial atoms of the seed
Lie long concealed ere they exert the breed;

And after sundry ages past, produce
The tardy likeness of the latent juice.
Hence families such different figures take,
And represent their ancestors in face, and hair, and
    make;
Because of the same seed, the voice, and hair,
And shape, and face, and other members are,
And the same antique mould the likeness does
    prepare.
Thus oft the father's likeness does prevail
In females, and the mother's in the male;
For since the seed is of a double kind,
From that where we the most resemblance find,
We may conclude the strongest tincture sent,
And that was in conception prevalent.

   Nor can the vain decrees of powers above
Deny production to the act of love,
Or hinder fathers of that happy name,
Or with a barren womb the matron shame;
As many think, who stain with victims' blood
The mournful altars, and with incense load,
To bless the showery seed with future life,
And to impregnate the well-laboured wife.
In vain they weary heaven with prayer, or fly
To oracles, or magic numbers try;
For barrenness of sexes will proceed
Either from too condensed, or watery, seed:
The watery juice too soon dissolves away,
And in the parts projected will not stay;

The too condensed, unsouled, unwieldy mass,
Drops short, nor carries to the destined place;
Nor pierces to the parts, nor, though injected home,
Will mingle with the kindly moisture of the womb.
For nuptials are unlike in their success;
Some men with fruitful seed some women bless,
And from some men some women fruitful are,
Just as their constitutions join or jar:
And many seeming barren wives have been,
Who after matched with more prolific men,
Have filled a family with prattling boys;
And many, not supplied at home with joys,
And found a friend abroad to ease their smart,
And to perform the sapless husband's part.
So much it does import that seed with seed
Should of the kindly mixture make the breed;
And thick with thin, and thin with thick should join,
So to produce and propagate the line.
Of such concernment too is drink and food,
To incrassate, or attenuate the blood.

   Of like importance is the posture too,
In which the genial feat of love we do;
For as the females of the four-foot kind
Receive the leapings of their males behind,
So the good wives, with loins uplifted high,
And leaning on their hands, the fruitful stroke may
   try:
For in that posture will they best conceive;
Not when, supinely laid, they frisk and heave;

For action motions only break the blow,
And more of strumpets than of wives they show,
When answering stroke with stroke, the mingled
  liquors flow.
Endearments eager, and too brisk a bound,
Throws off the plough-share from the furrowed
  ground;
But common harlots in conjunction heave,
Because 'tis less their business to conceive
Than to delight, and to provoke the deed;
A trick which honest wives but little need.
Nor is it from the gods, or Cupid's dart,
That many a homely woman takes the heart,
But wives well-humoured, dutiful, and chaste,
And clean, will hold their wandering husbands fast;
Such are the links of love, and such a love will last.
For what remains, long habitude, and use,
Will kindness in domestic bands produce;
For custom will a strong impression leave.
Hard bodies, which the lightest stroke receive,
In length of time will moulder and decay,
And stones with drops of rain are washed away.

If for thyself thou wilt not watch thy whore,
Watch her for me that I may love her more;
What comes with ease we nauseously receive,
Who but a sot would scorn to love with leave?
With hopes and fears my flames are blown up higher,
Make me despair and then I can desire.
Give me a jilt to tease my jealous mind,
Deceits are virtues in the female kind.
Corinna my fantastic humour knew,
Played trick for trick and kept herself still new;
She, that next night I might the sharper come,
Fell out with me, and sent me fasting home;
Or some pretence to lie alone would take,
Whene'er she pleased her head and teeth would ache,
Till having won me to the highest strain,
She took occasion to be sweet again.
With what a gust, ye gods, we then embraced!
How every kiss was dearer than the last!
    Thou whom I now adore, be edified,
Take care that I may often be denied.
Forget the promised hour, or feign some fright,
Make me lie rough on bulks each other night.
These are the arts that best secure thy reign,
And this the food that must my fires maintain.
Gross easy love does like gross diet pall,
In queasy stomachs honey turns to gall.
Had Danae not been kept in brazen towers,

Jove had not thought her worth his golden showers.
When Juno to a cow turned Io's shape,
The watchman helped her to a second leap.
Let him who loves an easy Whetstone whore
Pluck leaves from trees, and drink the common shore.
The jilting harlot strikes the surest blow,
A truth which I by sad experience know.
The kind poor constant creature we despise,
Man but pursues the quarry while it flies.
　　But thou dull husband of a wife too fair,
Stand on thy guard, and watch the precious ware;
If creaking doors or barking dogs thou hear,
Or windows scratched, suspect a rival there;
An orange-wench would tempt thy wife abroad,
Kick her, for she's a letter-bearing bawd;
In short be jealous as the devil in Hell,
And set my wit on work to cheat thee well.
The sneaking city cuckold is my foe,
I scorn to strike but when he wards the blow.
Look to thy hits, and leave off thy conniving,
I'll be no drudge to any wittol living;
I have been patient and foreborn thee long,
In hope thou wouldst not pocket up thy wrong;
If no affront can rouse thee, understand
I'll take no more indulgence at thy hand.
What, ne'er to be forbid thy house and wife!
Damn him who loves to lead so dull a life.
Now I can neither sigh, nor whine, nor pray,
All those occasions thou hast ta'en away.

Why art thou so incorrigibly civil?
Do somewhat I may wish thee at the devil.
For shame be no accomplice in my treason,
A pimping husband is too much in reason.
    Once more wear horns before I quite forsake her,
In hopes whereof I rest thy cuckold-maker.

How blest is he, who leads a country life,
Unvexed with anxious cares, and void of strife!
Who studying peace, and shunning civil rage,
Enjoyed his youth, and now enjoys his age:
All who deserve his love, he makes his own,
And to be loved himself, needs only to be known.

  Just, good, and wise, contending neighbours come
From your award, to wait their final doom;
And, foes before, return in friendship home.
Without their cost, you terminate the cause;
And save the expense of long litigious laws
Where suits are traversed, and so little won,
That he who conquers, is but last undone.
Such are not your decrees; but so designed,
The sanction leaves a lasting peace behind,
Like your own soul, serene; a pattern of your mind.

  Promoting concord, and composing strife,
Lord of yourself, uncumbered with a wife;
Where, for a year, a month, perhaps a night,
Long penitence succeeds a short delight:
Minds are so hardly matched, that e'en the first,
Though paired by heaven, in paradise were cursed.
For man and woman, though in one they grow,
Yet, first or last, return again to two.
He to God's image, she to his was made;
So, farther from the fount, the stream at random strayed.

  How could he stand, when put to double pain,

He must a weaker than himself sustain!
Each might have stood perhaps; but each alone;
Two wrestlers help to pull each other down.

Not that my verse would blemish all the fair;
But yet, if *some* be bad, 'tis wisdom to beware;
And better shun the bait, than struggle in the snare.
Thus have you shunned, and shun the married state,
Trusting as little as you can to fate.

No porter guards the passage of your door
To admit the wealthy, and exclude the poor:
For God, who gave the riches, gave the heart
To sanctify the whole, by giving part:
Heaven, who foresaw the will, the means has wrought,
And to the second son, a blessing brought:
The first-begotten had his father's share;
But you, like Jacob, are Rebecca's heir.

So may your stores, and fruitful fields increase;
And ever be you blest, who live to bless.
As Ceres sowed, where'er her chariot flew;
As heaven to deserts rained the bread of dew,
So free to many, to relations most,
You feed with manna your own Israel host.

* * *

You hoard not health for your own private use,
But on the public spend the rich produce;
When, often urged, unwilling to be great,
Your country calls you from your loved retreat,
And sends to senates, charged with common care,
Which none more shuns, and none can better bear.

Where could they find another formed so fit
To poise with solid sense a sprightly wit?
Were these both wanting, (as they both abound)
Where could so firm integrity be found?

Well-born and wealthy, wanting no support,
Your steer betwixt the country and the court;
Nor gratify what'er the great desire,
Nor grudging give what public needs require.
Part must be left, a fund when foes invade;
And part employed to roll the watery trade;
E'en Canaan's happy land, when worn with toil,
Required a sabbath-year to mend the meagre soil.

* * *

O true descendant of a patriot line,
Who, while thou sharest their lustre, lendst them
thine,
Vouchsafe this picture of thy soul to see;
'Tis so far good as it resembles thee:
The beauties to the original I owe,
Which when I miss, my own defects I show.
Nor think the kindred muses thy disgrace;
A poet is not born in every race.
Two of a house, few ages can afford,
One to perform, another to record.
Praiseworthy actions are by thee embraced;
And 'tis my praise to make thy praises last.
For e'en when death dissolves our human frame,
The soul returns to heaven, from whence it came,
Earth keeps the body, verse preserves the fame.

TO SIR GODFREY KNELLER

Once I beheld the fairest of her kind,
And still the sweet idea charms my mind:
True, she was dumb; for nature gazed so long,
Pleased with her work, that she forgot her tongue;
But, smiling, said – She still shall gain the prize;
I only have transferred it to her eyes.
Such are thy pictures, Kneller, such thy skill,
That nature seems obedient to thy will;
Comes out, and meets thy pencil in the draft,
Lives there, and wants but words to speak her
   thought.
At least thy pictures look a voice; and we
Imagine sounds, deceived to that degree,
We think 'tis somewhat more than just to see.

   Shadows are but privations of the light;
Yet when we walk, they shoot before the sight;
With us approach, retire, arise, and fall;
Nothing themselves, and yet expressing all.
Such are thy pieces, imitating life
So near, they almost conquered in the strife;
And from their animated canvas came,
Demanding souls, and loosened from the frame.

   Prometheus, were he here, would cast away
His Adam, and refuse a soul to clay;
And either would thy noble work inspire,
Or think it warm enough, without his fire.

   But vulgar hands may vulgar likeness raise;

This is the least attendant on thy praise:
From hence the rudiments of art began;
A coal, or chalk, first imitated man:
Perhaps the shadow, taken on a wall,
Gave outlines to the rude original;
Ere canvas yet was strained, before the grace
Of blended colours found their use and place,
Or cypress tablets first received a face.

By slow degrees the godlike art advanced;
As man grew polished, picture was enhanced:
Greece added posture, shade, and perspective,
And then the mimic piece began to live.
Yet perspective was lame, no distance true,
But all came forward in one common view:
No point of light was known, no bounds of art;
When light was there, it knew not to depart,
But glaring on remoter objects played;
Not languished and insensibly decayed.

Rome raised not art, but barely kept alive,
And with old Greece unequally did strive;
Till Goths and Vandals, a rude northern race,
Did all the matchless monuments deface.
Then all the muses in one ruin lie,
And rhyme began to enervate poetry.
Thus in a stupid military state,
The pen and pencil find an equal fate.
Flat faces, such as would disgrace a screen,
Such as in Bantam's embassy were seen,
Unraised, unrounded, were the rude delight

Of brutal nations, only born to fight.

Long time the sister arts, in iron sleep,
A heavy sabbath did supinely keep;
At length, in Raphael's age, at once they rise,
Stretch all their limbs, and open all their eyes.

Thence rose the Roman, and the Lombard line,
One coloured best, and one did best design.
Raphael's, like Homer's, was the nobler part,
But Titian's painting looked like Virgil's art.

Thy genius gives thee both; where true design,
Postures unforced, and lively colours join,
Likeness is ever there; but still the best,
(Like proper thoughts in lofty language dressed,)
Where light, to shades descending, plays, not strives,
Dies by degrees and by degrees revives.
Of various parts a perfect whole is wrought;
Thy pictures think, and we divine their thought.

Shakespeare, thy gift, I place before my sight;
With awe I ask his blessing ere I write;
With reverence look on his majestic face;
Proud to be less, but of his godlike race.
His soul inspires me, while thy praise I write,
And I, like Teucer, under Ajax fight;
Bids thee, through me, be bold; with dauntless breast
Contemn the bad, and emulate the best.
Like his, thy critics in the attempt are lost;
When most they rail, know then, they envy most.
In vain they snarl aloof, a noisy crowd,
Like women's anger, impotent and loud.

While they their barren industry deplore,
Pass on secure, and mind the goal before,
Old as she is, my muse shall march behind,
Bear off the blast, and intercept the wind.
Our arts are sisters, though not twins in birth,
For hymns were sung in Eden's happy earth;
By the first pair, while Eve was yet a saint,
Before she fell with pride and learned to paint.
Forgive the allusion: 'twas not meant to bite,
But satire will have room where'er I write.
For oh, the painter muse, though last in place.
Has seized the blessing first, like Jacob's race.
Apelles' art an Alexander found,
And Raphael did with Leo's gold abound;
But Homer was with barren laurel crowned.
Thou hadst they Charles a while, and so had I;
But pass we that unpleasing image by.
Rich in thyself, and of thyself divine,
All pilgrims come and offer at the shrine.
A graceful truth thy pencil can command;
The fair themselves go mended from thy hand.
Likeness appears in every lineament,
But likeness in thy work is eloquent.
Though nature there her true resemblance bears,
A nobler beauty in thy piece appears.
So warm thy work, so glows the generous frame,
Flesh looks less living in the lovely dame.
  Thou paint'st as we describe, improving still
When on wild nature we engraft our skill,

But not creating beauties at our will.

Some other hand perhaps may reach a face,
But none like thee a finished figure place:
None of this age, for that's enough for thee,
The first of these inferior times to be,
Not to contend with heroes' memory.

Due honours to those mighty names we grant,
But shrubs may live beneath the lofty plant:
Sons may succeed their greater parents gone;
Such is thy lot, and such I wish my own.

But poets are confined in narrower space,
To speak the language of their native place;
The painter widely stretches his command,
Thy pencil speaks the tongue of every land.
From hence, my friend, all climates are your own,
Nor can you forfeit, for you hold of none.
All nations all immunities will give
To make you theirs, where'er you please to live;
And not seven cities, but the world, would strive.

Sure some propitious planet then did smile,
When first you were conducted to this isle;
Our genius brought you here, to enlarge our fame,
For your good stars are everywhere the same.
Thy matchless hand, of every region free,
Adopts our climate, not our climate thee.

Great Rome and Venice early did impart
To thee the examples of their wondrous art.
Those masters, then but seen, not understood,
With generous emulation fired thy blood;

For what in nature's dawn the child admired,
The youth endeavoured, and the man acquired.

That yet thou hast not reached their high degree,
Seems only wanting to this age, not thee.
Thy genius, bounded by the times, like mine,
Drudges on petty drafts, nor dare design
A more exalted work, and more divine.
For what a song, or senseless opera,
Is to the living labour of a play;
Or what a play to Virgil's work would be,
Such is a single piece to history.

But we, who life bestow, ourselves must live;
Kings cannot reign, unless their subjects give;
And they who pay the taxes bear the rule:
Thus thou sometimes art forced to draw a fool;
But so his follies in thy posture sink,
The senseless idiot seems at last to think.
Good heaven! that sots and knaves should be so vain
To wish their vile resemblance may remain
And stand recorded, at their own request,
To future days, a libel or a jest!

Meantime, whilst just encouragement you want,
You only paint to live, not live to paint.

Else should we see your noble pencil trace
Our unities of action, time, and place;
A whole composed of parts, and those the best,
With every various character expressed;
Heroes at large, and at a nearer view;
Less, and at distance, an ignobler crew;

While all the figures in one action join,
As tending to complete the main design.
　More cannot be by mortal art expressed,
But venerable age shall add the rest:
For time shall with his ready pencil stand,
Retouch your figures with his ripening hand,
Mellow your colours, and embrown the taint,
Add every grace, which time alone can grant;
To future ages shall your fame convey,
And give more beauties than he takes away.